ROBOTIC WARFARE

ROBOTIC WARFARE

Edited by

Dr. R.K. Pruthi

PRASHANT PUBLISHING HOUSE

DELHI

Published by

PRASHANT PUBLISHING HOUSE
C-34, 28 Futa Road, Gali No. 3
West Karawal Nagar
New Delhi-110094
Ph.: 011-22963970
(M) : 9810396373

Robotic Warfare

First Published 2009

ISBN 978-81-90644-8-9

PRINTED IN INDIA

Published by

CONTENTS

PREFACE

Robotic technologies will change the future of warfare. The military robotic system will proliferate throughout the twenty first century force structure. The future battlefield will be inhabited by a growing number and kind of robots.

Therefore, the aim of the book is to provide our readers current innovative and up to date material on this profoundly important subject.

For preparing this work we have incurred indebtedness of internationally reputed authorities on this subject of immense importance and their scholarly articles. We record our respectful acknowledgment to them and appreciation for kind cooperation from librarians.

My publisher assisted by his team of dedicated colleagues, by publishing this valuable material in its present form, for further and deeper intellectual adventures, have earned the love and patronage of my readers, whose satisfaction with the work will be our biggest reward.

Editor

1

ROBOTIC WARFARE

Long range planning to prepare for modern warfare includes developing robotics for military use.

Several countries are inducting robots for Military Warfare. A new generation of Military Robots are being devised. New Military robots are undergoing a shift in their structure and missions. They are being designed to become lighter and more agile. This will enable them to move easily and quickly to the designed spots.

Thus a robotic development, starting with completely human controlled system and ending with autonomous, armed cooperative robots. But with what final results? Do you want to know all this and more?

A robot is a *mechanical* or *virtual, artificial agent*. It is usually a system, which, by its appearance or movements, conveys a sense that it has *intent* or *agency* of its own. The word robot can refer to both physical robots and virtual software agents, but the latter are usually referred to as *bots* to differentiate. While there is still discussion about which machines qualify as robots, a typical robot will have several, though not necessarily all of the following properties:

- is not *'natural'* i.e. artificially created
- *can sense* its *environment*, and *manipulate* or *interact* with things in it
- has some ability to make choices based on the environment, often using automatic control or a preprogrammed sequence.
- is *programmable*
- moves with one or more axes of *rotation* or *translation*
- makes **dexterous** coordinated movements
- appears to have intent or agency (See *anthropomorphism* for examples of ascribing intent to inanimate objects.)

Defining Characteristics

The last property, the appearance of agency, is important when people are considering whether to call a machine a robot, or just a machine. In general, the more a machine has the appearance of agency, the more it is considered a robot.

Mental Agency

For robotic engineers, the physical appearance of a machine is less important than the way its actions are *controlled.* The more the control system seems to have agency of its own, the more likely the machine is to be called a robot. An important feature of agency is the ability to make choices. So the more a machine could feasibly choose to do something different, the more agency it has. For example:

- a clockwork car is never considered a robot.[7]
- a remotely operated vehicle is sometimes considered a robot. (or *telerobot*).

- a car with an onboard computer, like *Bigtrak,* which could drive in a programmable sequence might be called a robot.
- a *self-controlled car,* like the 1990s *driverless cars* of *Ernst Dickmanns,* or the entries to the *DARPA Grand Challenge,* which could sense its environment, and make driving decisions based on this information would quite likely be called robot.
- a *sentient* car, like the fictional *KITT,* which can make decisions, navigate freely and converse fluently with a human, is usually considered a robot.

Physical Agency

However, for many *laymen,* if a machine looks *anthropomorphic or zoomorphic* (e.g. ASIMO or *Aibo*), especially if it is *limb*-like (e.g. a simple *robot arm*), or has limbs, or can move around, it would be called a robot.

For example, even if the following examples used the same control architecture:

- a player piano is rarely characterized as a robot[9]
- a *CNC* milling machine is very occasionally characterized as a robot.
- a *factory automation arm* is almost always characterized as a robot or an industrial robot.
- an autonomous wheeled or tracked device, such as a self-guided rover or self-guided vehicle, is almost always characterized as a robot, a mobile robot or a service robot
- a zoomorphic mechanical toy, like *Roboraptor,* is usually characterized as a robot.

- a humanoid, like *ASIMO*, is almost always characterized as a robot or a service robot.

Interestingly, while a 3-axis CNC milling machine may have a very similar or identical control system to a robot arm, it is the arm which is almost always called a robot, while the CNC machine is usually just a machine. Having a limb can make all the difference. Having eyes too gives people a sense that a machine is aware ("the eyes are the windows of the soul"). However, simply being anthropomorphic is not sufficient for something to be called a robot. A robot must do something, whether it is useful work or not. So, for example, a rubber dog chew, shaped like ASIMO, would not be considered a robot.

Official definitions and classifications of robots

There are many variations in definitions of what exactly is a robot. Therefore, it is sometimes difficult to compare numbers of robots in different countries. To try to provide a universally acceptable definition, the *International Organisation for Standardization* gives a definition of robot in *ISO 8373,* which defines a robot as "an automatically controlled, reprogrammable, multipurpose, manipulator programmable in three or more axes, which may be either fixed in place or mobile for use in industrial automation applications." This definition is to be used when comparing the number of robots in each country.

In spite of the ISO definition, countries, such as the USA and Japan have different definitions of robots. Japan, for example, lists very many robots partly because more machines are counted as robots. Since both Japan and the USA are important players in the development of robotics, the definitions used in these countries will be mentioned.

Robotics Institute of America

The Robotics Institute of America (RIA) defines a robot as:

A re-programmable multifunctional manipulator designed to move materials, parts, tools, or specialized devices through variable programmed motions for the performance of a variety of tasks.

The RIA recognizes four classes of robot:

1 Handling devices with manual control

2 Automated handling devices with predetermined cycles

3 Programmable, servo-controlled robots with continuous of point-to-point trajectories

4 Robots capable of Type C specifications which also acquire information from the environment for intelligent motion

Japanese Robot Association

The *Japanese Robot Association* (JARA) classifies robots into six classes:

1 Manual - Handling Devices actuated by an operator

2 Fixed Sequence Robot

3 Variable-Sequence Robot with easily modified sequence of control

4 Playback Robot, which can record a motion for later playback

5 Numerical Control Robots with a movement program to teach it tasks manually

6 Intelligent robot: that can understand its environment and able to complete the task despite changes in the operation conditions

Other definitions of robot

There is no one definition of robot which satisfies

everyone, and many people have their own. For example, *Joseph Engelberger,* a pioneer in industrial robotics, once remarked: "I can't define a robot, but I know one when I see one."

Etymology

A scene from *Karel Capek's* 1920 play *R.U.R. (Rossum's Universal Robots),* showing three robots.

The word *robot* was introduced to the public at large by *Czech* writer *Karel Capek* in his play *R. U.R. (Rossum's Universal Robots),* which premiered in 1921.[The play begins in a *factory* that makes 'artificial people'—they are called *robots,* but are closer to the modern idea of *androids* or even *clones,* creatures who can be mistaken for humans. They can plainly think for themselves, though they seem happy to serve. At issue is whether the "Robots" are being *exploited* and, if so, what follows? (See also *Robots in literature* for details of the play).

However, Karel Capek himself was not the originator of the word; he wrote a short letter in reference to an article in the *Oxford English Dictionary* etymology in which he named his brother, painter and writer Josef Capek, as its actual inventor.[18] In an article in the Czech journal *Lidove noviny* in 1933, he also explained that he had originally wanted to call the creatures *labofi* (from *Latin labor,* work). However, he did not like the word, seeing it as too artificial, and sought advice from his brother Josef, who suggested "roboti".

The word *robot* comes from the word *robota* meaning literally *serf labor*, and figuratively "drudgery" or "hard work" in *Czech, Slovak* and *Polish*. The origin of the word is the *Old Church Slavonic rabota* "servitude" ("work" in contemporary *Bulgarian* and *Russian*), which in turn comes from the *Indo-European* root **orbh. Robot* is cognate with the **German** word *Arbeiter* (worker).

History

Cadmus Sowing the Dragon's teeth, *by Maxfield Parrish,* 1908

Ancient Developments

The idea of artificial people dates at least as far back as the ancient legends of *Cadmus*, who sowed dragon teeth that turned into soldiers, and the myth of *Pygmalion*, whose statue of Galatea came to life. In *Greek mythology*, the deformed god of metalwork (Vulcan or Hephaestus) created mechanical servants, ranging from intelligent, golden handmaidens to more utilitarian three-legged tables that could move about under their own power, and the robot *Talos* defended *Crete*. Medieval *Persian alchemist Jabir ibn Hayyan* included recipes for creating artificial snakes, scorpions, and humans in his coded *Book of Stones*. *Jewish* legend tells of the *Golem*, a clay creature animated by *Kabbalistic* magic. Similarly, in the *Younger Edda, Norse mythology* tells of a clay giant, Mokkurkalfi or Mistcalf, constructed to aid the troll Hrungnir in a duel with *Thor*, the God of *Thunder*.

In *ancient China*, a curious account on automata is found in the *Lie Zi* text, written in the 3rd century BC. Within it there is a description of a much earlier encounter between *King Mu of Zhou (1023 BC-957 BC)* and a mechanical engineer known as Yan Shi, an 'artificer'. The latter proudly presented the king with a life-size, human-shaped figure of his mechanical handiwork.

The king stared at the figure in astonishment. It walked with rapid strides, moving its head up and down, so that anyone would have taken it for a live human being. The artificer touched its chin, and it began singing, perfectly in tune. He touched its hand, and it began posturing, keeping perfect time...As the performance was drawing to an end, the robot winked its eye and made advances to the ladies in attendance, whereupon the king became incensed and would have had Yen Shih [Yan Shi] executed on the spot had not the latter, in mortal fear, instantly taken the robot to pieces to let him see what it really was. And, indeed, it turned out to be only a construction of leather, wood, glue and lacquer, variously coloured white, black, red and blue. Examining it closely, the king found all the internal organs complete—liver, gall, heart, lungs, spleen, kidneys, stomach and intestines; and over these again, muscles, bones and limbs with their joints, skin, teeth and hair, all of them artificial...The king tried the effect of taking away the heart, and found that the mouth could no longer speak; he took away the liver and the eyes could no longer see; he took away the kidneys and the legs lost their power of locomotion. The king was delighted.

Concepts akin to a robot can be found as long ago as the 4th century BC, when the Greek mathematician *Archytas* of Tarentum postulated a mechanical bird he called "The Pigeon" which was propelled by *steam*. Yet another early *automaton* was the *clepsydra,* made in 250 BC by *Ctesibius* of *Alexandria,* a physicist and inventor from *Ptolemaic Egypt. Hero of Alexandria* (10-70 AD) made numerous innovations in the field of automata, including one that allegedly could speak.

Medieval Developments

Al-Jazari (1136-1206), an *Arab Muslim inventor* during the *Artuqid dynasty,* designed and constructed a number of automatic machines, including kitchen appliances, musical automata powered by *water,* and the first *programmable humanoid robot* in 1206. Al-Jazari's robot was a boat with four automatic musicians that floated on a lake to entertain guests at royal drinking parties. His *mechanism* had a programmable drum machine with *pegs* (*cams*) that bump into little *levers* that operate the *percussion.* The drummer could be made to play different rhythms and different drum patterns by moving the pegs to different locations.[22]

One of the first recorded designs of a humanoid robot was made by *Leonardo da vinci* (1452-1519) in around 1495. Da Vinci's notebooks, rediscovered in the 1950s, contain detailed drawings of a mechanical *knight* able to sit up, wave its arms and move its head and jaw. The design is likely to be based on his anatomical research recorded in the *Vitruvian Man*. It is not known whether he attempted to build the robot (see: *Leonardo's robot*).

Early Modern Developments

An early *automaton* was created in 1738 by *Jacques de Vaucanson*, who created a mechanical duck that was able to eat and digest grain, flap its wings, and excrete.

The Japanese craftsman *Hisashige Tanaka*, known as "Japan's Edison," created an array of extremely complex mechanical toys, some of which were capable of serving tea, firing arrows drawn from a quiver, or even painting a Japanese *kanji* character. The landmark text *Karakuri Zui (Illustrated Machinery)* was published in 1796. (T. N. Hornyak, *Loving the Machine: The Art and Science of Japanese Robots* [New York: Kodansha International, 2006])

In *1898 Nikola Tesla* publicly demonstrated a radio-controlled (teleoperated) boat, similar to a modern ROV. Based on his patents *U.S. Patent 613,809, U.S. Patent 723,188* and *U.S. Patent 725.605* for "teleautomation", Tesla hoped to develop the wireless *torpedo* into a *weapon system* for the *US Navy*. (Cheney 1989).

Modern Developments

In the 1930s, *Westinghouse Electric Corporation* made a humanoid robot known as *Elektro*, exhibited at the *1939* and *1940 World's Fairs*.

The first electronic *autonomous robots* were created by *William Grey Walter* of the Burden Neurological Institute at Bristol, *England* in *1948* and *1949*. They were named *Elmer* and *Elsie*. These robots could sense light and contact with external objects, and use these stimuli to navigate.

It wasn't until the second half of the *twentieth century*, when *integrated circuits* were invented, and computers began to double rapidly in power (roughly every two years according to *Moore's Law*), that it became possible to build robots as we imagine them. Until that time, automatons were the closest things to robots, and while they may have looked humanoid, and their movements were complex, they were not capable of the self-control and decision making that robots are today.

The first truly modem robot, digitally operated, programmable, and teachable, was invented by *George Devol* in 1954 and was ultimately called the *Unimate*. It is worth noting that not a single patent was cited against his original robotics patent (*U.S. Patent 2,988,237*). The first Unimate was personally sold by Devol to *General Motors* in *1960* and installed in *1961* in a plant in *Trenton, New Jersey* to lift hot pieces of *metal* from a *die casting* machine and stack them.[21]

Robot Fatalities

The first human to be killed by a robot was *Robert Williams* who died at a casting plant in *Flat Rock, MI (January 25, 1979)*.

A better known case is that of 37-year-old *Kenii Urada*, a Japanese factory worker, in 1981. Urada was performing routine maintenance on the robot, but neglected to shut it down properly, and was accidentally pushed into a *grinding machine*.

Timeline

Date	Significance	Robot Name	Inventor
Third century B.C.	Automata activated by clocks at preset times		Ctesibius of Alexandria
Third century B.C.	During a parade organized by Ptolemy II Philadelphus, a statue of Nysa could stand up by itself from a sitting position, pour libations of milk and sit down again.		Ctesibius of Alexandria?
First Century A.D.	In two works (Pneumatica and Automata) Heron of Alexandria describes many machines and automata (mainly from previous sources)		Ctesibius of Alexandria, Philo of Byzantium, Heron of Alexandira
1206	First programmable hum anoid robot with four automatic musicians	Mechanical boat	Al-Jazari
~1495	Early design of a humanoid robot	mechanical knight	Leonardo da Vinci
1738	Early automaton, a mechanical duck that was able to eat grain, flap its wings, and excrete.	The Digesting Duck	Jacques de Vaucanson
1920	Word robot coined.		Josef Capek
1921	The term "robot" used in a play called "R.U.R." or "Rossum's Universal Robots"		Karel Capek
1930s	Early humanoid robot. It was exhibited at the 1939 and 1940 World's Fairs	Elektro	Westinghouse Electric Corporation
1942	The word *robotics* appears in the science fiction short story I, Robot.		Isaac Asimov
1948	Simple robots which exhibitbiological like behaviours.	Elsie and Elmer	William Grey Walter

(Contd...)

Date	Significance	Robot Name	Inventor
1954	Patent submitted for first digitally controlled robot and first teachable robot, (U.. Patent 2,988,237)		George Devol
1956	First robot company, Unimation, is founded by Geogre Devol and Josephy Engelberger based on Devol's seminal patents; first commercial robot.	Unimate	Geogre Devol
1956	Phrase *artificial intelligence* is coined at a conference in Dartmouth. Massachusetts.		Mary in Minsky and John McCarthy
1961	First industrial robt installed.	Unimate	
1963	First Palletizing Robot.		Fuji Yusoki Kogyo
1973	First robot with six electromechanically driven axes, known as FAMULUS.	Kuka	
1975	Programmable Universal Manipulation Army (a Unimation product)	Programmable Universal Machine for Assembly	Victor Scheinman
1979	Robert Williams, an American factory worker, is killed by a robot.		
2000	A humanoid robot that can recognize human faces, see stereoscopically, walk and run on different types of ground (including stairs), and respond (in words and in actions) to English and Japanese commands.	ASIMO	Honda Corporation

Contemporary Uses

Main articles: *Industrial robot* and *Domestic robot*

Robots can be placed into roughly two categories based on the type of job they do:

- Jobs which a robot can do better than a human. Here, robots can increase productivity, accuracy, and endurance.
- Jobs which a human could do better than a robot, but it is desirable to remove the human for some reason. Here, robots free us from dirty, dangerous and dull tasks.

Increased Productivity, Accuracy, and Endurance

Pick and Place robot, Contact Systems C5 Series

Jobs which require speed, accuracy, reliability or endurance can be performed far better by a robot than a human. Hence many jobs in factories which were traditionally performed by people are now robotized. This has led to cheaper mass-produced goods, including automobiles and electronics. Robots have now been working in factories for more than fifty years, ever since the Unimate robot was installed to automatically remove hot metal from a die casting machine. Since then, factory automation in the form of large stationary manipulators has become the largest market for robots. The number of installed robots has grown faster and faster, and today there are more than 1 million robots in operation worldwide (Half of the robot population is located in Asia, 1/3 in Europe, and 16% in North America. Australasia and Africa each account for 1 %.).

German *KUKA Industrial robots* doing vehicle under body assembly.

Some examples of factory robots:

- **Car production:** This is now the primary example of

factory automation. Over the last three decades automobile factories have become dominated by robots. A typical factory contains hundreds of *industrial robots* working on fully automated production lines one robot for every ten human workers. On an automated production line a vehicle chassis is taken along a conveyor to be *welded, glued, painted* and finally assembled by a sequence of robot stations.

- **Packaging: Industrial robots** are also used extensively for palletizing and packaging of manufactured goods, for example taking drink cartons from the end of a conveyor belt and placing them rapidly into boxes, or the loading and unloading of machining centers.
- **Electronics:** Mass produced *printed circuit boards* (PCBs) are almost exclusively manufactured by pick and place robots, typically with *SCARA* manipulators, which remove tiny *electronic components* from strips or trays, and place them on to PCBs with great accuracy. Such robots can place several components per second (tens of thousands per hour), far outperforming a human in terms of speed, accuracy, and reliability.

Help Mate trackless pharmacy bot navigates autonomously to transport drugs, lab specimens, supplies and medical records.

- **Automated Guided Vehicles (AGVs):** Mobile robots, following markers or wires in the floor, or using vision or lasers, are used to transport goods around large facilities, such as warehouses, container ports, or hospitals. Early AGV style robots were limited to tasks that could be accurately defined and must be performed the same every time. Very little feedback or intelligence was required, and the robots may need only the most basic of *exteroceptors* to sense things in their environment, if any at all. However, newer AGV's, such as the Speci-Minder, ADAM, Tug, and

PatrolBot Gofer qualify under the JARA definition of intelligent robots. They use some form of natural features recognition to navigate. Scanning lasers, stereovision or other means of sensing the environment in two- or three-dimensions is combined with standard deadreckoning calculations in a probabilistic manner to continuously update the AGV's current location, eliminating cumulative error. This means that the SelfGuided Vehicle (SGV) can navigate a space autonomously once it has learned it or been provided with a map of it. Such new robots are able to operate in complex environments and perform non-repetitive and non-sequential tasks such as carrying tires to presses in factories, delivering masks in a semi-conductor lab, delivering specimens in hospitals and delivering goods in warehouses.

Dirty, Dangerous, Dull or Inaccessible Tasks

The *Roomba* domestic *vacuum cleaner* robot does a menial job

There are many jobs which a human could perform better than a robot but for one reason or another the human either does not want to do it or cannot be present to do the job. The job may be too boring to bother with, for example domestic *cleaning;* or be too dangerous, for example exploring inside a *volcano.* These jobs are known as the "dull, dirty, and dangerous" jobs. Other jobs are physically inaccessible. For example, exploring another planet, cleaning the inside of a long pipe or performing *laparoscopic* surgery.

- **Robots in the home:** As their price falls, and their performance and computational ability rises[47], making them both affordable and sufficient)! autonomous, robots are increasingly being seen in the home where they are taking on simple but unwanted jobs, such as *vacuum cleaning,* floor cleaning and *lawn mowing.* While they have been on the market for several years, 2006 saw a great increase in the number of domestic robots sold. By 2006, *iRobot* had sold more than 2 million vacuuming robots. They tend to be relatively autonomous, usually only requiring a command to begin their job. They then proceed to go about their business in their own way. At such, they display a good deal of agency, and are considered intelligent robots.

A *laparoscopic* robotic *surgery* machine.

- **Telerobots:** When a human cannot be present on site to perform a job because it is dangerous, far away, or inaccessible, teleoperated robots, or telerobots are used. Rather than following a predetermined sequence of movements a telerobot is controlled from a distance by a human operator. The robot may be in another room or another country, or may be on a very different scale to the operator. A *laparoscopic surgery* robot such as *da Vinci* allows the surgeon to work inside a human patient on a relatively small scale compared to open surgery, significantly shortening recovery time. An interesting use of a telerobot is by the author *Margaret Atwood,* who has recently started using a robot pen (the Longpen) to sign books remotely. The Longpen is similar to the *Autopen* of the *1800s.* This saves the financial cost and physical inconvenience of traveling to book signings around the world.[49] At the other end of the spectrum, Robot Connecter robot is designed to be used by anyone to stay in touch with family or friends from far away. One robot in use today, In touch health's RP-7 remote presence robot, is being used by doctors to communicate with patients, allowing the doctor to be anywhere in the world. This increases the number of patients a doctor can monitor.
- **Military robots:** Teleoperated robot aircraft, like the Predator *Unmanned Aerial Vehicle,* are increasingly being used by the military. These robots can be controlled from

anywhere in the world allowing an army to search terrain, and even fire on targets, without endangering those in control. Many of these robots are teleoperated, but others are being developed that can make decisions automatically; choosing where to fly or selecting and engaging enemy targets.[51] Hundreds of robots such as *iRobot's Pack bot* and the *Foster-Miller* **TALON** are being used in *Iraq* and *Afghanistan* by the *U.S. Military* to defuse roadside bombs or *Improvised Explosive Devices* (IEDs) in an activity known as Explosive Ordnance Disposal (EOD).*Autonomous robots* such as MDARS and Seekur are being developed to perform security and surveillance tasks at military facilities to address manpower shortages as well as keeping troops out of harm's way. The Crusher Unmanned Ground Vehicle (UGV) is being developed to perform military missions autonomously.

- **Elder Care:** The population is *aging* in many countries, especially Japan, meaning that there are increasing numbers of elderly people to care for but relatively fewer young people to care for them. Humans make the best carers, but where they are unavailable, robots are gradually being introduced.

Unconventional Robots

Much of the research in robotics focuses not on specific industrial tasks, but on investigations into new types of robot, alternative ways to think about or design robots, and new ways to manufacture them. It is expected that these new types of robot will be able to solve real world problems when they are finally realized.

A nanocar made from a single molecule

Nanorobots: Nanorobotics is the still largely hypothetical technology of creating machines or robots at or close to the scale of a *nanometer* (10-9 *meters*). Also known as *nanobots or nanites,* they would be constructed from *molecular machines.* So far, researchers have mostly produced only parts of these complex systems, such as bearings, sensors, and Synthetic *molecular* motors, but functioning robots have also been made such as the entrants to the Nanobot Robocup contest. Researchers also hope to be able to create entire robots as small as *viruses* or *bacteria,* which could perform tasks on a tiny scale. Possible applications include micro surgery (on the level of individual cells), utility fog, manufacturing, weapon and cleaning. Some people have suggested that if there were nanobots which could reproduce, the earth would turn into "grey goo", while others argue that this hypothetical outcome is nonsense.

- **Soft Robots:** Most man-made machines are made from hard, stiff materials, especially *metal* and *plastic.* This is in contrast to most *natural organisms,* which are mostly *soft tissues.* Researchers at *Tufts University* recently developed robots with *silicone* bodies and flexible actuators (*air muscles, electroactive polymers, ferrofluids*). The control software emphasizes soft behaviors using fuzzy logic and neural networks.

Soft-bodied robots can look, feel, and behave differently from traditional hard robots, enabling new applications. Some of these robots are currently exhibited at the *Museum of Modern Art* (MoMa) in New York City.

Molecubes in motion

- **Reconfigurable Robots:** A few researchers have investigated the possibility of creating robots which can alter their physical form to suit a particular task, like the fictional *T -1000.* Real robots are nowhere near that sophisticated however, and mostly consist of a small number of cube shaped units, which can move relative to their neighbours, for example *SuperBot.* Algorithms have been designed in case any such robots become a reality.

A swarm of robots from the Open-source micro-robotic project.

- Swarm robots: Inspired by *colonies of insects* such as *ants* and *bees,* researchers hope to create very large swarms (thousands) of tiny robots which together perform a useful task, such as finding something hidden, cleaning, or spying. Each robot would be quite simple, but the *emergent behaviour* of the swarm would be more complex. The whole set of robots can be considered as one single distributed system, in the same way an ant colony can be considered a *superorganism.* They would exhibit *swarm intelligence.* The largest swarms so far created include the iRobot swarm, and the *Open-source micro-robotic project* swarm, which are being used to research collective behaviors. Swarms are also more resistant to failure. Whereas one large robot may fail and ruin the whole mission, the swarm can continue even if several robots fail. This makes them attractive for space exploration missions, where failure can be extremely costly.

- **Evolutionary Robots:** is a *methodology* that uses *evolutionary computation* to help design robots, especially the body form, or motion and behaviour *controllers.* In a similar way to *natural evolution,* a large population of robots is allowed to compete in some way, or their ability to perform a task is measured using a *fitness function.* Those that perform worst are removed from the population, and replaced by a new set, which have new behaviors based on those of the winners. Over time the population improves, and eventually a satisfactory robot may appear. This happens without any direct programming of the robots by the researchers. Researchers use this method both to create better robots, and to explore the nature of evolution.[71] Because the process often requires many generations of robots to be simulated, this technique may be run entirely or mostly in simulation, then tested on real robots once the evolved algorithms are good enough.

Virtual Reality: Robotics also has application in the design of **virtual reality** interfaces. Specialized robots are in widespread use in the haptic research community. These robots, called "haptic interfaces" allow touch-enabled user interaction with real and virtual environments. Robotic forces allow simulating the mechanical properties of "virtual" objects, which users can experience through their sense oftouch.

Dangers and Fears

Although current robots are not believed to have developed to the stage where they pose any threat or danger to society, fears and concerns about robots have been repeatedly expressed in a wide range of books and films. The principal theme is the robots' intelligence and ability to act could exceed that of humans, that they could develop a conscience and a motivation to take over or destroy the human race. (See *The Terminator, Runawav, Robocop,* the Replicators in *Stargate,* the Cylons in *BattleStar Galactica,* The Matrix, and 1. *Robot.)* Robots could be dangerous if they were programmed to kill or if they are programmed to be so smart that they make their own software, build their own hardware to upgrade themselves or if they change their own source code.

Frankenstein (1818), often called the first science fiction novel, has become synonymous with the theme of a robot or monster advancing beyond its creator. Probably the best known author to have worked in this area is *Isaac Asimov* who placed robots and their interaction with society at the center of many of his works. Of particular interest are Asimov's *Three Laws of Robotics.* Currently, malicious programming or unsafe use of robots may be the biggest danger. Although industrial robots may be smaller and less powerful than other industrial machines, they are just as capable of inflicting severe injury on humans. However, since a robot can be programmed to move in different trajectories depending on its task, its movement can be unpredictable for a person standing in its reach. Therefore, most industrial robots operate inside a security fence which separates them from human workers. *Manuel De Landa* has theorized that humans are at a critical and significant juncture where humans have allowed robots, "smart missiles," and autonomous bombs equipped with artificial perception to make decisions about killing us. He believes this represents an important and dangerous trend where humans are transferring more of our cognitive structures into our machines. Even without malicious programming, a robot, especially a future model moving freely in a human environment, is potentially dangerous because of its large moving masses, powerful actuators and unpredictably complex behavior. A robot falling on someone or just stepping on his foot by mistake could cause much more damage to the victim than a human being of the same size. Designing and programming robots to be *intrinsically safe* and to exhibit safe behavior in a human environment is one of the great challenges in robotics. Some theorists, such as *Eliezer Yudkowsky,* have suggested that developing a robot with a powerful conscience may be the most prudent course of action in this regard.

Literature

Robots have frequently appeared as characters in works of literature. *Isaac Asimov* wrote many volumes of *science fiction* focusing on robots in numerous forms and guises, contributing greatly to reducing the *Frankenstein complex,* which dominated early works of fiction involving robots. His *three laws of robotics* have become particularly well known for codifying a simple set of behaviours for robots to remain at the service of their human creators.

The first reference in Western literature to mechanical servants appears in *The Iliad of Homer*. In Book XVIII,

Hephaestus, god of fire, creates new armour for the hero Achilles. He is assisted by robots. According to the *Rieu* translation, "Golden maidservants hastened to help their master. They looked like real women and could not only speak and use their limbs but were endowed with intelligence and trained in handwork by the immortal gods." Of course, the words "robot" or "android" are not used to describe them, but they are nevertheless mechanical devices human in appearance.

Numerous words for different types of robots are now used in literature. Robot has come to mean mechanical humans, while *android* is a generic term for artificial humans. *Cyborg* or "*bionic* man" is used for a human form that is a mixture of organic and mechanical parts. Organic artificial humans have also been referred to as "constructs" (or "biological constructs").

In science fiction, the Three Laws of Robotics are a set of three rules written by Isaac Asimov, which almost all positronic robots appearing in his fiction must obey. Introduced in his 1942 short story "Runaround", although foreshadowed in a few earlier stories, the Laws state the following:

1. A robot may not injure a human being or, through inaction, allow a human being to come to harm.
2. A robot must obey orders given to it by human beings except where such orders would conflict with the First Law.
3. A robot must protect its own existence as long as such protection does not conflict with the First or Second Law.

Later, Asimov added the Zeroth Law: "A robot may not harm humanity, or, by inaction, allow humanity to come to harm"; the rest of the laws are modified sequentially to acknowledge this.

According to the Oxford English Dictionary, the first passage in Asimov's short story "Liar!" (1941) that mentions the First Law is the earliest recorded use of the word robotics. [1] Asimov was not initially aware of this; he assumed the word already existed by analogy with mechanics, hydraulics, and other similar terms denoting branches of applied knowledge.

Due in part to Asimov's Robot stories, robotic characters have since become a staple of science fiction, appearing in a variety of print and cinematic works including *Star Trek, Star Wars*, and *Doctor Who*.

Competitions and Exhibitions .

Competitions for robots are gaining popularity, attracting participation from amateurs, private industry, schools and research institutions. Robots compete at a wide range of tasks including destructive combat[77], non-destructive combat, fire-fighting, maze solving, performing tasks, navigational exercises (eg. the *DARPA Grand Challenge*) and many others. Some contests[81] require participants to provide tutorials showing how they built and programmed their robot.

Here is an alphabetical list of ongoing, successful competitions and exhibitions.

Botball is a *LEGO*-based competition between fully *autonomous* robots. There are two divisions. The first is for high-school and middle-school students, and the second (called "Beyond Botball") is for anyone who chooses to compete at the national tournament. Teams build, program, and blog about a robot for five weeks before they compete at the *regional* level. Winners are awarded *scholarships* to register for and travel to the national tournament. Botball is a project of the KISS Institute for Practical Robotics, based in Norman, Oklahoma.

The *DARPA Grand Challenge* has held events since 2004 testing *driverless cars* in obstacle courses.

The *First Robotics Competition* (FRC) is a multinational competition that teams professionals and young people to solve an engineering design problem. These teams of mentors (corporate, teachers, or college students) and high school students collaborate in order to design and build a robot in six weeks. This robot is designed to playa game that is developed by *FIRST* and changes from year to year. FIRST, or For Inspiration and Recognition of Science and Technology, is an organization founded by inventor *Dean Kamen* in 1992 as a way of getting high school students involved in and excited about engineering and technology.

FIRST LEGO League (FLL) is a robotics competition for elementary and middle school students (ages 9-14, 9-16 in Europe), arranged by FIRST. Each year the contest focuses on a different topic related to the sciences. Each challenge within the competition then revolves around that theme. The students then work out solutions to the various problems that they're given and meet for regional tournaments to share their knowledge and show off their ideas. The World Festival is held every year in Atlanta.

The FIRST Tech Challenge (FTC) is a mid-level **robotics** competition targeted toward high-school aged students. It offers the traditional challenge of a FIRST competition but with a more accessible and affordable robotics kit. The ultimate goal of FTC is to reach more young people with a lower-cost, more accessible opportunity to discover the excitement and rewards of science, technology, and engineering.

The Intelligent Ground Vehicle Competition (IGVC) has hosted a yearly student robotics competition every year since 1993, usually in Michigan and usually in early June. See the web site for dates and location. It is multidisciplinary, theory-based, hands-on, team-implemented, outcome-assessed, and based on product realization. Many of the participants design their vehicles during year-long course work.[citation needed] Students in business and engineering management, language and graphic arts, and public relations also participate.[citation needed] Students solicit and interact with industrial sponsors who provide component hardware and advice, and in that way get an inside view of industrial design and opportunities for employment.[citation needed]

The *International Robot Exhibition* (IREX), organized by the *Japan Robot Association* (lARA), has run biennially since 1973.

The *Trinity College Fire-Fighting Robot Contest* competition in April 2007 was the 14th annual event. There are many different divisions for all skill levels. Robots in the competition are encouraged to find new ways to navigate through the rooms, put out a candle and save a "child" from a building. Robots can be composed of any materials, but must fit within certain size restrictions.

Previous and Future Competitions and Exhibitions

The British TV show *Robot Wars*, in which machines built by amateur hobbyists battle to destroy one another, ran from 1997 to 2003. The machines, however, were radio controlled and had little autonomy.

Robots in Warfare

The use of *robots* in *warfare*, although traditionally a topic for *science fiction*, is being researched as a possible future means of fighting *wars*. Already several *military robots* have been developed by various armies.

Some believe the future of modern warfare will be fought by automated weapons systems [1] The *U.S. Military* is investing heavily in research and development towards testing and deploying increasingly automated systems. The most prominent system currently in use is the unmanned aerial vehicle (*IAI Pioneer & RQ-l Predator*) which can be armed with Air-to-Ground missiles and remotely operated from a command centre in reconnaissance roles. *DARPA* has hosted competitions in 2004 & 2005 to involve private companies and universities to develop unmanned ground vehicles to navigate through rough terrain in the *Moiave Desert* for a final prize of $2 Million [2]. The field of artillery has also seen some promising research with an experimental weapons system named *"Dragon Fire II"* [3] which automates the loading and ballistics calculations required for accurate predicted fire, providing a 12 second response time to artillery support requests. However, weapons of warfare have one limitation in becoming fully autonomous: there remain intervention points which requires human input to ensure that targets are not within restricted fire areas as defined by *Geneva Conventions* for the laws of war.

There have been some developments towards developing autonomous fighter jets and bombers [4]. The use of autonomous fighters and bombers to destroy enemy targets is especially promising because of the lack of training required for robotic pilots, autonomous planes are capable of performing maneuvers which couldn't otherwise be done with human pilots (due to high amount of G-Force), plane designs don't require a life support system, and a loss of a plane doesn't mean a loss of a pilot. However, the largest draw back to robotics is their inability to accommodate for non-standard conditions. Advances in *artificial intelligence* in the near future may help to recitfy this, but this also raises the ethical issue of whether it is safe to leave military ordnance in the hands of a non-human intelligence.

2

OPTIONS TO MODERN WARFARE

Currently there are many different robotic *options* available to *modern militaries*. Robots can begun by wire from a distance, run by remote control, steered thru tele-robotics or semi or fully autonomously. There are plenty of *"fire and forget"* weapons, dumb weapons and smart munitions as well. The line between categories is often blurred with steerable big-gun rounds, aircraft swarm UAV control and Tele-robotic machines which can fire thru human command or by way of software rules that include target identification and firing.

How fast is this technology moving? Very fast as we noted the first fully autonomous vehicles made it thru a grueling course set up by **DARPA**. Contestants in the *Grand Challenge* borrowed technologies from any industry they could find them and thanks to all the various sponsors of all the teams, they too learned a thing or two.

These companies and industry sponsors will enjoy the findings of their research and the transfer technologies that come forth in the future. Such new technologies into the marketplace will increase efficiency and productivity. But that is just the start as these technologies will save tens or thousands of lives on our Nation's Highways thru SmartCar Systems and Net-Centric Automobiles of the future.

There have been many *Military Contracts awarded for robotic systems* in the United States, some have already been introduced to the modern battlespace and there will be many more to follow. Including fully autonomous logistic convoys, submarines, ground combat vehicles and more UAV models and all these future promises have already been outlined in the Army's Future Force and Air Force Road Maps. Many are fully funded in the Nation's budget.

Quite a few other allied nations have also added robotic unmanned vehicles monies to their budgets and rightfully so. Allied nations must protect against rogue nation technologies, International Terrorists sponsored by rogue nation-states and technologies sold to rogue nations by quasi-friendly super powers. As the technology of robotic warfare progresses so to will the technologies of our declared and undeclared enemies, our future potential enemies and their aligned rogue-alities.

Robots in the Modern Battlespace

Today the United States has many robotic fighting tools in theatre that are used every day, from the predator drones to the ***anti-IED robotic bomb squad units***. There are hand-held UAVs as well. Currently being tested along our borders and in *Iraq and Afghanistan* are technologies I am not at liberty to discuss at this time, perhaps it will be all public knowledge in the near future. Indeed it does not take a rocket-scientist to figure it out, one only needs to read the defense industry rags from around the Globe and apply just a little imagination. This of course is only the beginning.

As smart as these Future Fighting Force tools are they are only going to become smaller, more robust in capability and more prolific in numbers as they help determine the outcome of conflicts. Even the enemy is working frantically to copy our use of robotics and although their *remote detonation of road side bombs,* car bombs and other incendiary devices are rudimentary, it often unfortunately serves its purpose. Using cell phones, ***Sony Play Station*** parts and other available electronics this is indeed a mild form of robotic usage also.

Hezbollah, Ramas and Iran have all used UAV surveillance. *Hezbollah shocked Israel* when they used a radar-guided missile to attack a war ship during the *Lebanon Conflict*. Some believed the technology to be Chinese, perhaps some Israeli technology, which was sold to the Chinese, repackaged to Iran and given to Hezbollah. Either way the International Terrorists, insurgency in Iraq and even *Al Qaeda* is not without some modern robotic technology.

Proper use of robotic technology solves many problems in our military. It is estimated that for every soldier or airmen on the frontline or participating at the tip of the sword there are 20-25 military personal throughout the command & control and logistical supply chain. Military robotics clearly increases efficiency and productivity - delivering more for less and with pinpoint accuracy. The Future Fighting Force roadmaps are dead on target with regards to the use of robotics on the battlefield and none of this is not by accident. They are designing the future of war and changing the paradigm of political impasse, warfare tactics and military engagement protocol.

Now then, it should be noted that less than 1% of all the humans who have ever lived have died in war. Although we hear more about the deaths in war today due to the far-reaching and often biased media the truth is that major fighting is concluded quite quickly with much less collateral damage thanks to smart munitions. This does not make armed conflict less devastating for those involved, yet it must be considered when discussing the reality of war technology. Indeed, just because allied forces can fight with unheard of precision does not mean the enemy will not attack pure civilian soft targets to promote their will or radical notions.

There is and has always been a good bit of the national budget of any nation, spent on its military, as it is important to protect all they are and all they have built.

Wouldn't you? Indeed and so we all do, both friend and foe. Due to the huge amount of expenditures there are always many companies and entrepreneurs willing and ready to work on research and development of war toys. Yet, the business of war is not a game and the stakes are very high - *self preservation* of a nation being amongst the top rationals.

Robotic Technology on, above and below the battle field has come a long way in the last couple of decades and yet this is only the beginning. Coming soon will be many new applications such as robotic units to pick up the wounded and take them to military medical facilities. There will also be **MAVs or Micro-Air Vehicles** perhaps capable of swarming like insects. Bird sized MAVs are already nearly ready for service. Fully autonomous perimeter security mobile robots with weapons attached are already being deployed. *Underwater Unmanned Vehicles* are also in production with some units already in the water.

Unmanned Vehicles

"Future Rules of Engagement"

The idea of robots sent to *annihilate the enemy* is troubling for many to contemplate, especially after watching some of the *Hollywood Movies* of the last couple decades. Some ask what if they malfunction, yet could it really be any worse than human soldiers who in the past have raped and pillaged? It is a fact of war, in past periods it was accepted, the spoils of war, today it is not acceptable, but it happens. Will robots left to their own recognizance be any less problematic with their rules of engagement?

Indeed one has to ask if one side uses robots who is to say the other side will have as sophisticated of robots which will have better *artificial intelligent software* able to discern friendly, non-combatant, enemy or foe? Who makes this decision and who is designing these systems and programming their software? Once all nations have such things should they agree on open source code as a way to level the battle field and protect innocent civilians? Open source code, ouch? What about hackers, can you imagine terrorist hackers in the future taking over entire robotic armies? And what if and when these systems are damaged who is to say if that mal-function may cause unnecessary death of civilians or initiate friendly fire? The question with robotic war fighters has been pondered; Who decides who lives or dies? Whether this question is answered soon or whether it takes time to render such a decision, the predicament and perplexing problem is here and it is here now.

Few would argue that terrorists should be eliminated by any and all means possible including robots or ***UAVs with Hell-Fire Missile Systems***. There have already been high-ranking military men and futurist philosophers contemplate this problem and the consensus appears to be that Robots should Not be allowed to kill humans unless a human being is in the loop, which seems to point towards the future of "Video Game Warfare" thru a tele-robotic motif. Then the robotic unmanned ground vehicle, system or VAV is nothing more than a tool at the hand of a human?

Should this be a rule that humans must be involved be added to the Geneva Convention? It appears that war treaties are rarely followed and the Geneva Conventions may be followed at the on-set, yet as a nation-state builds on its Nationalism thru religion and has labeled the enemy unfit to lead or live then they rationalize the breaking of the rules. Some say this is merely a survival mechanism since in *"True War"* are there any rules at all? *Kill or be killed* is often the only thought process that is working as the battles thicken and the stakes become higher.

If one side breaks the *Geneva Convention* in one area then is the other side justified in casting aside all the rules or should it be more like a sporting event with penalities? As the reciprocal responses escalate can we really expect any such rules over robotic warfare and robots engaging humans on their own accord to be meaningful? After all one can easily argue that a *human programmed the machine* in the first place and therefore it is still a hand tool of war.

Does a Bomber Pilot really know where the dumb bombs will land? Does Hezbollah as it sends 2,000 rockets into Israel knowing they will be hitting innocent civilians really care? Will such rules whether sponsored by the UN, NATO or agreed upon in advance by all nations amount to anything worthy? And to that point in the heat of battle when one side is over powered, will they not pull out all the stops? Currently there are all sorts of rules on Chemical, Biological and Nuclear weapons, yet it seems these are often in the arsenals of all Nation's Militaries today.

We have all heard the saying; *All is fair in Love and War.* Indeed it is amazing how many people believe just that and in the heat of battle ones strict adherence to rules will be challenged more often than not. What about ***Isaac Asimov's*** famous Robot Rules? (source: WikiPedia).

The Three Laws of Robotics:

1. A Robot may not injure a human being or, through inaction, allow a human being to come to harm.

2. A Robot must obey orders given to it by human beings except where such orders would conflict with the First Law.

3. A Robot must protect its own existence as long as such protection does not conflict with the First or Second Law.

Later a Fourth Law was added (The Zeroth Law):

4. A Robot may not harm humanity, or, by inaction, allow humanity to come to harm.

Apparently current military philosophers and thinkers are not the only ones contemplating the future reality and the use of robots in warfare. It appears that Isaac Asimov's rules for robots is totally out the window or perhaps we might say that the future force robots will soon be coming thru an international terrorist window near you?

International Terrorist Proxies and Rules

We already know that International Terrorist Organizations are using robotic technologies to wage war against the *"infidel"* or those who have a different belief system in the name of their god or so they proclaim. So far we know that UAVs mostly small aircraft model size are being used, but in the future they will certainly have unmanned ground vehicles and suicide bomber cars without the person. One advantage the International Terrorist enemy has is that there are plenty of folks that they are able to recruit to carry out such murders. Their *devaluation of human life* is already evident not only with the civilians they murder but with those who have joined them.

If rules are made in the future and it is agreed upon by all nations that robots can only kill other robots if autonomous or can kill human combatants only if there is a human pulling the trigger or in the loop, even if tele-robotically; we still cannot expect International Terrorists to play by such rules. After all, they purposely *cut-off the heads of their hostages* - clearly this is against the Geneva Conventions.

If International Terrorists have no nation-state of their own to be held accountable by the *International Community,* then we should not expect any of them playing by the rules. When rogue nation-states hire out International Terrorists to do their bidding we should not expect the rules to be followed either. If you are fighting an enemy on an uneven playing field, well this simply does not make any sense at all.

Can we therefore expect that their will be different rules of engagement for murderous International Terrorists who pride them selves in blowing up innocent civilians in schools, buses, trains, malls, office buildings or planes? And how do we deal with the nations who hire these criminals out, fund them and give them *WMD* or *robotic high-tech weapons*? Who is responsible in this case?

Enemies with US Unnmanned Technologies

Each time the US or one of our allies develops advances in robotic weapons of war there is a chance that these weapons will make it into the hands of our enemies. If a company sells weapons to another nation, which in-turn sells them to Iran and we know Iran to be sponsoring federational Terrorist Organizations then these weapons will be used against *US Troops in Iraq* or against the Jewish State of Israel or innocent civilians at soft targets such as Ferries, Public Gatherings, Train Stations, Critical Infrastructure or Commercial Aircraft.

Robotic Electronic Space Technologies will end up being used for weapons of war and to help guide weapons systems. If an Indian defense contractor sells robotic systems to Iran, they could very well end up killing US Troops. If India trades weapons technologies with Russia then Russia could easily incorporate them into the anti-aircraft systems it sells to Iran who in turn might give them to *Hamas* or *Hezbollah*. The International Weapons industry will find-ways to get technologies into the hands of those who are willing to pay for them.

The more difficult the transaction the higher the price and the more money involved for all the participants. Even if all these types of sales stopped, which they never will, still the amount of information flow and the number of spies in Nations producing such weapons technologies are huge. The *International Weapons Dealers Networks* reach around the globe and deals are made and rogue nations who desire such weapons and have the money, will succeed in acquisition.

Thus whatever weaponry in the robotic warfare realm that is produced will be available to friend and foe alike. Even if most nations agree to rules of engagement that are fair to humanity, war is still hell and in the end will anyone follow such rules, as there are *no points for second place*. If the US Defense Contractors sell to allied nations and some *quasi-friendly nations,* it still only takes a few side transactions and a little bit of reverse engineering before your top secret technology is in the hands of your most brutal enemies.

Some robotic defense technologies should be shared for peaceful endeavours and used for the common good, but we know all to well, that evil men and the innate characteristics of mankind will indeed intervene and they will be used against his fellow man. ***Self-Driving Transportation*** *could be used for many things increasing the flows of human civilization.* Eventually these technologies will be available to free-enterprise for commercial uses. The sooner the better in order to save lives, but just like nuclear power, we know all to well what mankind's first use for this technology was and it was not pretty. War never is.

Hide and Seek Strategies

In the age of robotic mobile missile launchers and autonomous or tele-robotic border patrol sentry units any defending nation, which anticipates a surprise attack will strategically place their weaponry to protect it from the incoming attack. Tactics such as camouflage and turning off electronic signatures will be employed. We know from Gulf War I and Gulf War II that the opposing military often attempted to hide their military equipment inside of structures, behind buildings or dug into the local terrain. Indeed none of this is too surprising - it is just using caution to better the odds.

As weapons become more sophisticated and satellites are able to pre-map the terrain, the slightest change will trigger an anomaly and alert the opposing force of a potential target, a dead give away for sure. Still in this day and age of mobile robotic defense a cat and mouse game can be employed to prevent destruction of defense assets. It is hard to hide from the latest sophisticated spy-satellites, as much of the technology can even find oil far below the Earth's surface, thus finding an iron army tank or mobile track missile launcher is not too tough.

The mobility of the unit does provide at least a small level of advantage against the sophisticated systems that nations like the United States now employ, but is it enough? Case in point might be Iran's Russian bought mobile missile launching systems VS a 22,000 sortie US Strike.

They say that in major tank battles in the current paradigm of the Net-Centric Battlespace; once the battle begins the life expectancy of a tank and its crew is just around 2 minutes. Of course with robotic weaponry there will be no humans in the tank, mobile missile launcher or border perimeter robotic sentry. Still any nation investing is such high-tech war toys knows that they are very expensive and must have systems aboard to prevent their earlier destruction in the very first round of battle or the initial attack.

For such a piece of military hardware to survive it must remain undetected for as long as possible. This means no heat, no electronic signature, no movement, no changes in terrain, which is easier said than done. Indeed, we are asking these units to be invisible to all modern day sensors and also to the human eye. Is this even possible?

Fooling the Sensors

"Decoy and Deception"

There is no doubt that the stakes are very high for the defending nation and any mistake or failure to understand the opposing force and their ability to be "all knowing" in the modern battlespace bubble will result in severe losses and perhaps their most important defense barriers. One new technology which will change and tilt the scale of favor slightly towards the defending nation are the new materials such as carbon composites and vehicles made out of predominantly nano-tube structure. Some current sensors on strike aircraft might have trouble finding them, however generally the targets, their locations and type are already pre-known prior to the striking aircraft's mission. However being mobile insures fluidity of motion and a slight advantage.

The goal in the first series of strikes is to eliminate Surface-to-Air threats and the US Navy and US Air Force are extremely proficient at this. Older hardware such as tanks, mobile missile launchers and vehicles made of steel and iron really will not be able to maintain their concealment in today's battlefield; *They are Toast*, as ready room participants often say.

Other strategies will also be considered by the defending nation; "If" the military mobile defense systems are made of hard to see materials, well hidden from view, will turn off all electronic and allow the engines to cool completely they will render little if any heat signature. Is it therefore possible for them to *remain somewhat hidden?* Somewhat is not good enough in the modern battles pace or the new paradigm of warfare.

If something sits too long it will show up as an anomaly on the Spy Satellite and if it moves too often it will have a heat signature and perhaps a CO_2 plume which also shows up under various spectrums of light. What if the vehicles were electric? Indeed, this makes sense too, but electric motors also get hot and take a little while to cool as well and they will need to power up a motor of some type at sometime to re-charge. Even if they were solar powered, they would still require large solar panels thus giving away their position.

This does somewhat remind us of the saying; *"No where to run, no where to hide!"* Of course this is the goal of the opposing strike force. When a defending nation is in such a position, it makes their political will and demands somewhat fruitless, as if push comes to shove and political impasse rears its head then there is always hell to pay.

Of course the striking force has the element of surprise and this is a huge advantage and as long as the intelligence is tight, this is a feather in their cap. The striking force will also employ various tactics such as running decoys to get the mobile missile launchers to *"turn on"* and as soon as they do, they become instant targets or are painted for the real strike force which cometh. Although we have not seen small UAVs illuminating as larger targets in swarms, we will.

One problem is that 10,000 men scattered across a thousand square miles might sit and wait with shoulder launch surface-to-air missiles, although generally these are only good for a few miles. A man portable unit does create risk for the striking force, although many of the smart munitions will be dropped from much higher altitudes and therefore these weapons are not viable to prevent the striking force from taking out mobile missile launchers or fixed SAM sites or defense system.

A nation defending itself may attempt to use shoulder launched surface-to-air missiles to prevent first strike although this will most likely lead to more robust anti-personal weapons being dropped strategically from the air. So that might not be such a smart move. Indeed, a defending army might be better off to hold onto those weapons until after the first strike, because the first strike will probably be very successful and thus they will need these weapons for later.

In Vietnam often the striking force would encounter hundreds of people lying on the ground and firing straight up as the aircraft flew over on their bombing runs shooting nothing more than small arms (guns). Did this work? Not often, but it goes to show you to what lengths armies will go to defend their infrastructure, equipment or nation.

The defending army will often set up decoys and employ deception tactics also, much like the striking force. In fact they might set up a sued pick-up truck with junk in the back under a not so perfect camouflage cover, knowing the striking force will consider it a target and as the striking force comes in, they are picked up in a trap. As great as these types of decoy strategies might have worked in past periods, one must understand that the sophisticated military hardware of today allows an eagle eye view of the situation and such a tactic could back fire completely.

Of course all too often an army will underestimate their competitor and thus pay the ultimate price. The mission of the striking force is to eliminate the enemy's defense systems, crush their communication infrastructure and then hit the main objective targets. In a full-scale war there will be many targets and thus it might take 72 hours to hit them all, most likely not, but it is possible that the major fighting in a modern war could last that long.

Total War or complete annihilation of all life and complete surrender can take much longer as the human slaughter rages on. It is a gruesome spectacle, but is a fact of human history. Robotic rapid warfare might indeed speed things up and actually produce far fewer human civilian casualties.

One more recent tactic being implemented by some rogue combatants and rogue nation-states is to use *human shields,* knowing the striking force will have to deal with the media backlash in the event they attempt to hit the target anyway. Luckily with very accurate smart munitions, this will not always work, but sometimes the tactic does work, for instance an enemy command and control which is located in the basement underneath a civilian school, hospital, religious location or apartment complex.

The civilians normally do not have a choice, if they protest they will be killed and so either way they are needless victims. Of course if a defending army no longer values the lives of its citizens more the reason for continuation of the strike to institute regime change for the sake of human rights and humanitarian causes.

Indeed the media is being used as a tactic of deception in modern wars and human conflict. Although often enough the media becomes extremely limited after an electronic attack and after communication of the enemy is completely defunct. This brings up another point of contention, if the media is aiding the enemy and prolonging the conflict then more needless human life will occur, thus is the *media to be amongst the first targets?* Some say yes, others deplore the concept. I stand neutral for I am not a General, but, I do value human life and thus would tend to consider ALL options.

The other issues with regards to media is that their communication systems also show up as electronic signatures and must be isolated by the striking force, if possible and if not possible perhaps more of a reason to eliminate all possible treats to insure a quick, decisive and complete victory. (NFP).

Other interesting new tactics are Infrared Heat Signature decoys which will mimic the heat of a soldier, combustion engine, ship or just engine aircraft. Scattering such decoy systems to fool the enemy does make sense especially as both the striking offensive force and the sitting duck defense army plots its battle strategies.

New uniforms are already being developed to keep body heat signatures to a minimum, vehicles are being specially coated and the heat from exhaust being rerouted and reused to make energy. Stealth aircraft also spread out the heat from the exhaust, these simple strategies and more will continue to be used and these technologies will continue to evolve.

Fiber Optic Ground Vehicle Strategies

In previous wars the radar systems to locate enemy aircraft were located away from the antiaircraft SAM sites. The enemy would leave the radar system off until the aircraft were very close and then flip the switch to turn it on, paint the target and then launch, as soon as possible. This made it hard for the striking force to find the target without using itself as bait, quite a deadly game of cat and mouse. With mobile missile launchers the defending nation believes it has the advantage and whereas it does have *"an" advantage* it does not have *"the" advantage* and there is a huge difference.

Currently some nations are developing *robotic mobile anti-aircraft missile launchers* which have a very long fiber optic cable. The robotic missile launcher will be displaced to predetermined locations and rotate its position every three or four days. The robot will stick a antenna stake in the ground which will allow communication with its tele-robotic operator and then unwind a 1/2 to 1 mile long cable as it goes. Any communication electronic signature will show up at the stake and not at the mobile missile launcher. Provided the unit has excellent camouflage and cover, it *might* greatly increase its survival rate.

One of the systems being designed now uses 3G + wireless phone technologies, but the defending nation must realize that those wireless phone towers will be first on the list as targets, because the potential disruptions of the cell-tower plume and cellular signals by stealth fighter might be enough to help track them or might help track terrain following stealth unmanned combat aerial vehicles (UCAVs).

Tele-robotics left without communication just leaves one more sitting duck target for the striking forces. These technologies need to be re-thought completely. Tele-robotic systems in the battles pace make sense if you are in control of the communications system, but when you are the defender under attack from a modern strike force, that is the first thing that goes - all your communication and thus collapse of command and control, chaos and loss of the battle.

Additionally, as defense contractors work to perfect these tele-robotic systems and the fiber optic line separation to prevent electronic signatures, U AVs are being developed with optical flow sensors to locate straight line anomalies which can see the line strewn out. A small low level UAV might seek and destroy or fly over to the robotic mobile missile launcher and drop off a hand grenade or become a single mission UAVs with an aboard destruct on impact device.

Since multiple sensors such a lidar, radar, infrared, optical and sonar will be used by both the invading strike team and the defending army, even if the electronic signature is removed, the heat signature and satellite anomaly are still active.

> *You can fool some of the sensors some of the time,*
> *but you cannot fool all the sensors all of the time..*

Although I have not heard any discussion on this topic it might make sense for the defending army to string multiple fiber optic lines from multiple directions and coat the fiber optic lines with the local color for camouflage, then use frequency hopping or skipping with the tele-robotic communication system.

If one antenna is hit, it will simply stop being used by the system and the remaining antennas will be used. With multiple targets all around the area will appear to be a hot bed of activity and attract the invading forces closer—*"Trap Door Spider" technique.*

Indeed, of course the more computer advanced striking force would design artificial intelligence to estimate the location of the units based on how the antennas were laid out and send in seek and destroy loitering smart munitions. Once the target launches to hit *"the seek and destroy"* drone, it will be identified as a target and thus immediately eliminated. *Next*!

If the defending army attempted to do this then the system might be viable to for a small nationstate against an unsophisticated attacker. Yet, even Iran, which has added the *"old junk"* used Russian Missile Launchers to its defense systems, which have *active matrix RFID satellite tags* hidden and embedded inside so they can be tracked and identified by US Satellites as practice targets; well it simply will not work against a sophisticated striking force. Indeed with spy satellites which find anomalies in Earth's surface height of over 2 feet, even a new retaining wall shows up on the images and the artificially intelligent computers finds these within hours.

Even if you can fool most of the sensors most of the time, good back fooling the satellite by day or by night!

What if the Solar Flares knock out the spy satellites? Well this is not likely, but even if. They did the *Stealth UAVs* can see the ground and their imaging is even truer than those of the satellites. There is really no way to hide old iron and steel mobile Russian missile launchers, indeed this is why the Russians sold them to Iran you see? Whether they are robotic or driven by men hell-bent in dying in battle for their god is irrelevant, they will not escape elimination from the battlefield.

What about a new low to the ground mobile missile launcher made out of carbon composite and electrically powered from a fuel cell? Well, unfortunately there is the heat signature issue again, as *during the conversion process fuel cells generate quite a bit of heat.* If the heat is kept at bay, then perhaps this might be possible if the unit is low to the ground in a flat shape, although if it is too flat it will not be able to get over rough terrain and if it stays on the roads it will get picked up either way. If the unit gets stuck or it runs out of juice, like a sitting duck until destroyed.

What about a self-burrowing robotic mobile missile launcher made out of composite that runs on an electric motor? Well, ha ha ha, yes, yes, indeed, there is always another way. Of course it takes a lot of power to bury such a unit and while it would be safe underground from electronic attack for the most part, it may not be able to un bury itself in time to help in the defense of the nation-state. If something like this is ever developed it will most likely be done in the United States where they have the research and development budget to do so. Good point.

Now if 1000s of these could be buried and hooked to fiber optic lines with antennas away from their position they most likely could survive the onslaught of the aggressor, but it is difficult to undertake such a project without someone noticing and thus the striking force would avoid this area until after the war and then go collect all this buried electronic treasure. If the aggressor knows of this thru intelligence gathering of other geo-spatial analysis, they might adopt a much more robust set of first strike weaponry such as nuclear or an MOAB type scenario.

Electronic Attack (EA)

Electronic Attack is an option of modern first strike military action, but it is not always the best option. This is because if you go too heavy handed and take out All the electronics, then it will be difficult to intercept transmission for Intelligence Gathering or use the electronic transmissions as homing beacons to pick secondary targets. One error that is often made as nations reach a political impasse and stop talking is that the rhetoric heats up and some nations over boast their military defense systems.

Often this leads to an over kill approach for not only over powering the defending nations electronic defense systems but literally taking out all the electronic systems in the entire country. One of the major flows of any civilization is the flow of communication and when it disappears the nation-state will be on the verge of collapse even without the war going on. Chaos and Controversy does assist in warfare, but it also leads to additional problems later on. A Generals goal is to win and indeed his major concerns are with his team not the opposing force.

Quelling the communication of Command and Control of the enemy and basic public communication that they might use makes sense. Taking out reciprocal defense systems is a must to win the battle and if the enemy generals are listening to local media to follow the battle, perhaps shutting that down might also be wise. Of course if it is shut down no one can use it for propaganda and thus the striking force will need to bring their own news broadcasting systems.

One last ditch tactic of a nation-state defending itself might be to take out "all" communication on both sides, for instance attempt to "flash" the satellites and send a large rocket up very high with a huge electromagnetic pulse or many such rockets simultaneously. The goal here would be to remove all communication and render the smart munitions useless, wipe out Aircraft Carrier Communication, remove local AWACS and net-centric battlespace communication systems and hope to fight a more old style war with what ever the defending nation has left in the way of military equipment and hardware.

Would such a strategy work? Well, for a while, but remember that Aircraft Carriers have all sorts of back up systems and are protected and submarines could surface and be used in their place by way of relay. AWACS could be fully operational with new units in 4-6 hours. Aircraft below the deck of the air craft carrier would be still in tact and could be launched in a very short time period. As our Think Tank ran all these scenarios, the amount of redundancy and capabilities of the present US systems would be up to 90% within such a short proximity that it would be a very bad move for the defending army. Of course desperate folks do desperate things and you just never know. Perhaps this is why the US Military is ready for these sorts of things?

The reality is that the defending nation-state does not have a chance against a couple of aircraft carriers and a fully-integrated net-centric battles pace using all the modern day technology. It is not a fair fight. Of course war is not really fair anyway. Even if the defending nation got the upper hand even for a brief moment, if the US military ever did pull out all the stops, there truly would not be anything left to discuss after all the dust settled. Each time we ran all the potential eventualities in our war game scenarios, we found similar results in the end, as the US Military captured the opposing forces King in an extremely short number of moves. Actually all in all it is pretty impressive and our scenarios were completely unbiased.

Even a Super Power like Russia or China with modern day advanced weapons and nuclear submarines, would have a tough go of it and in the end all scenarios show the Americans as prevailing and even with all the luck factored in the number of battles were extended only slightly and the war prolonged anywhere from a few additional hours to 1-2 days maximum.

The use of 15 to 20,000 robotic unmanned ground vehicles of the defending nation state only slightly added to the total number of sorties and number of smart munitions used, thus only adding 5-8 hours total to the air war. The cost to procure this many vehicles for a defensive system did not pan out and was a very poor use of military expenditures for the defending nation-state. However, for limited wars, border patrols or offense, the expenditures are more than justified, as our studies show. Striking forces on the other hand should procure such units.

If the unmanned ground vehicles were underground and hidden until after the first 72 hours of the initial attack (if possible), then the unmanned robotic ground vehicles of the defending nation state would serve well in defending against the ground war. However, it should be noted that after the major SAM sites are removed and the mobile missile launchers destroyed the helicopter gun ships and their highly mobile arsenal would render the robotic unmanned vehicles that were left rather useless.

Now then when a smaller nation-state was defending itself against another small nation-state without the fire-power of the United States or NATO combined, then 15,000 robotic unmanned vehicles are a very viable war toy. Thus any allied nation would be wise to own tens of thousands of them, but any rogue nation-state, challenging the Free-World would simply add fodder and targets to their own demise. Any nation attacking a small rogue nation which did not have NATO support could use robotic unmanned vehicles extremely effectively without maximum air-support and have an excellent chance for a full and quick victory, as long as they had a decent striking force air-campaign and the number of sorties needed the prior.

This author in no way is an advocate of robotic unmanned vehicles as the be all, end all of military hardware and yet with the rapid advances in this technology it is quite obvious that any serious military would be foolish not to leverage these assets in order to serve their political will, if such a challenge or crisis occurred.

Can Unmanned Robotic Ground Vehicles Be Shielded from Electronic Attack?

It appears that the answer is yes to a large degree with the proper use of materials. Carbon NanoTube Construction and perhaps lead atoms inside the carbon nano-tubes could encase the electronic brains of the UGV and thus protect it from EA. All of this is forth coming and there are rumors some of these protection cages with similar make ups in structure already exist. Any truly viable unmanned ground vehicle that was expected to survive must have a strategy to protect itself in such an environment and against such electronic weapons.

Swarming Robotic Strategies

For unmanned ground vehicles to be affective in the

modern battles pace, they must be able to work autonomously and together in teams. They will need to share data and be able to run semi-autonomously if the tele-robotic connection is broken. These unmanned vehicles like the modern UAVs will need to go into a safety mode and protect themselves and use artificially intelligent software and collaborative connections with other robots *on* the battle field to continue the mission.

Of course as these UGVs work together they will be up against UAVs from the enemy also working in swarms and networks. Currently there are many UGV - UAV team concepts where the two work together and share information for accurate target identification, acquisition and hunting. Theoretically speaking if command and control were eliminated by the enemy, the unmanned vehicles would carry out their previous orders until they could no longer do so. Of course military ethicists have all sorts of things to say about that concept, but it is intriguing to know that robots can fight the entire war once they are set lose on the battle field?

After Round One

Today's major conflicts consist of a hard fought a quick paced battle for the higher ground, indeed currently the highest ground is already owned by NATO forces and the United States and that would include Space. Yes, space, that is to say the satellites that help coordinate communication and the flow of information to the entire net-centric system. Indeed, eyes in the sky and AWACS are also in control of the high ground. Yet air-superiority and dominance allows attack aircraft and helicopter to control the battle.

Thus the first and foremost goal once the war starts is to control the air and eliminate the enemy's ability to advance or defend by constantly bombarding their positions. Before any of this happens of course the air must be secured for the aircraft to operate at low altitudes. Easier said than done as a defending army will have lots of military hardware on the ground that is a threat to the strike aircraft.

Strike aircraft operating in such scenarios early on try not to take too many risks, but war is war and they are there to do a job, a job that they are well-trained for. If the defending army has proper air-defense systems set up then they can attempt to stave off an attack, well as long as they can see the incoming attackers.

Yes, stealth and therefore you can see the challenge of defending ones nation against such technology. A successful offensive air-campaign these days is fought in hours not weeks or months. After round one, the air war, the battle field is much different.

In the air-war many tactics are used to eliminate SAM sites and major defensive equipment; then it is time to send in the ground teams. If the air-war has been fully executed and most all the major targets eliminated the ground war units can have ample close air-support for the rest of the battles. Since EA is used often sometimes the enemy is caught in a disarray and they are not functioning in any cohesive manner, this chaos adds opportunity to the attacking armies and their close air support assets.

This of is an excellent time for the advancing aggressive offensive army to employ robotic unmanned vehicles of its own to help in surveillance and securing area thru the use of high-tech sensors. Fast moving UGVs working with UAVs and tele-robotic human operators in mobile command centers or perhaps at a far-away location via satellite can cover a lot of ground and mop up without a huge amount of loss of life for the advancing offensive ground troops.

Electronic Attack
"What is Left to Fight"

Since part of fighting a successful initial air-war consists of disrupting the enemies supply lines, communication, command and control and its anti-aircraft defense systems electronic attacks are an important tactic. But once the defending army is rendered without such tools or military hardware after the first wave of sorties and any electronic attack, what is left for them to fight with? Often not much and as chaos ensues each sub-unit of the defending army is on it's own and without its prize military hardware that has been eliminated they are left to fight with little more than garden hand tools.

Most shoulder launched man-portable missiles are full of electronics and thus a strong electronic attack often renders the tiny missiles in the hand held tubes as duds. Shooting a dud at an attack plane or attack helicopter will most likely be the last thing that soldier does as the attack aircraft comes back around or the attack helicopter launches its own rockets in retaliation, by then it is too late to hide and too late to run.

At this point surrender might be a wise choice for the defending infantry that has survived up until this point, for some enemies with stronger nationalistic pride this maybe out of the question entirely. Thus the offensive armies will have to finish what has been started as the defending army is out of quarters. Still, in urban areas we notice that insurgencies and hold outs will use small arms, IEDs and rocket propelled grenades. Some cultures resort to suicide missions using whatever is available that they can find.

For all these reasons it makes sense to incorporate robotic unmanned systems to locate, detonate or deactivate roadside bombs using sensors, tele-robotics and sniffers. The advancing offensive army should do the responsible thing to cut down on losses using high-tech systems. Robotic Systems are already being used on unmanned ground vehicles to locate the direction of incoming fire from snipers and then return accurate fire to eliminate the threat (s).

Since the communication systems and perhaps power is out, operating in an urban setting can be challenging. Thus the offensive, policing or occupying force must re-establish communications without setting up vulnerable base camps that become an easy target for underground left over combatants.

Cell Phone Tower Dirigibles

Once the communication is knocked out the defending nation will lose much of its ability to execute its defense strategy against the attacking army. It will most likely lose all its capability to operate its tele-robotic unmanned vehicles as well, which considering the cost of acquisition, maintenance and replacement this is not pretty.

Worse think of the potential eventuality of the aggressor arm army capturing all these robotic fighting machines, swapping out chips and adding them as mobile robotic infantry to fight for their side against their owners? Without communication the defense army would be helpless to stop the robots and would be forced to fire upon them, eliminating those assets or be killed by them.

"The Robot of My Enemy is My Friend?"

Indeed the power to over ride, eliminate or infiltrate the enemy's communication system can work both ways. Perhaps the future of Military Hacking will be its own special command in the future. He who controls the robots and the electronics in the Net Centric Battlespace controls the battles and eventually wins the war. Once one competitor has the upper hand over the other it becomes paramount to regain communications. How can this be done?

Well there are many ways to regain communication and one way is to send up 3G Wireless Cell Towers inside dirigibles. Yes, they will become immediate targets and yet if the defending army had many of these small relay systems they could constantly send another one up. These units might be buried underground in advance just in case with trap doors which could be opened causing the system to inflate and float skyward.

Sounds crazy enough, but such systems have many advantages during chaos and one only has to imagine there current uses in dealing that aftermath of large Hurricanes or Typhoons. When all communication is wiped out the entire system could be run with instant up communication towers that could relay information to all the robotic search and rescue units.

If the systems were many and small and cheap to build they could be expendable and therefore usable in the battlespace too. If the aggressor assumed that the communication was knocked out they might attempt to try for hard to achieve targets and then be caught by surprise.

Of course if the aggressor army needed to bring in its own communication it might consider floating in its own communication systems on blimps, balloons or dirigibles. This could easily be done by using a UAV which had balloon bags with canisters that inflate when they reach the desired or designated area to provide communication to run all the unmanned ground vehicles. Of course this might be a back-up for satellites, ships, AWACS, UAV relays, mobile command centers, ground communication systems and/or base camps. It is that important because if you lose communication with your UGVs you might be in for a world of hurt.

Conclusions and Concepts

All nations should consider the use of military Unmanned Ground Vehicles and their various uses. Yet at the same time those in charge of such initiatives for future military assets must also be completely realistic of their capabilities, vulnerabilities and liabilities. It must be determined how they can best serve and when they should be deployed.

Fully autonomous fighting vehicle technologies are now available, yet problematic if they are to be counted on for defense or relied upon for offensive objectives when the stakes are high. It might well be possible that in the future these units are considered to be safer bet than the use of humans on-board the fighting vehicles and although that day is not here yet, it most certainly will be some day and some day soon. Unmanned Vehicles will change the future of warfare.

For tele-robotic unmanned ground vehicles the weak link is indeed the communication systems. Still more discussion, dialogue and strategizing will be needed to adapt to the new paradigm of robotic warfare. Electronic Attack and protecting against electronic attack must be considered. The future is now upon us, do you have a plan?

REFERENCES AND WORKS CITED

Background Reading Research Papers

1. Winslow, Lance. *Truck Technologies of the Future..* Online Think Tank Virtual Press. Palm Desert, CA. 2007
2. Winslow, Lance. *Hoverboards of the Future.* Online Think Tank Virtual Press. Palm Desert, CA. 2007
3. Winslow, Lance. *Holographic Technologies of the Future.* Online Think Tank Virtual, Press. Palm Desert, CA. 2007

RESEARCH PAPERS

1. Autonomous Vehicles in the Net-Centric Battlespace: http://spawar.navy.mil/robots/pubs/iuuvs 2000. pdf
2. Battlefield Information Integration: http://www.cs.unc.edu/~geom/WIHAVE/POSTERS/FINAL/hrl. pdf

3. Unmanned Tele-operated Robots as Medical Support: http://www.defence.gov.au/dpe/dhs/infocentre/publieations/journals/NoIDs/adihealth... apr05/ADFHealth 6 134 -3 8. pdf

4. Post Modern Terrorism - Foreign Affairs Magazine: http://ww.v.foreignaffairs.org/19960901faessay4222-faarticles/walter-laqueur/post.modern-terrorism-new-rules-for-an-old-game htmI

5. Terrorism Trends and Prospects - Rand Corp: https://www.rand org/pubs/monograph reports/MR989/R989.chap2. pdf

6. Fourth Wave - History of Terrorism: http://www.currenthistory.com/org pdf files/100/650/100 650 419.pdf

Section II

1. Where am I - Sensors and Methods for Mobile Robotic Positioning: http://www.eng.yale.edu/ee-labs/morse/other/pos96chl. pdf

2. Application of Radio Controlled Cars as Intelligent UGVs: http://phoenix.nmt.edu/~wedeward/papers/2004SPIEU GV. pdf

3. Summary or Articles of Visual Sensors in UGVs: http://csdI2.computer.org/comp/mags/co/2006/ 12/rz004. pdf

4. How UGVs Fail in the Field: http://crasar.csee.usf.edu/research/Publications/CRASAR-TR2004-16. pdf

5. Helping Maintain the Future Fighting Force - Sandia Labs: http://www.sandia.gov/news -center/publications/annual-report/ Fighting Force. pdf

6. UA Vs Future Fighting Force: http://www.me.wustl.edu/~aiaa/AIAA 2005 Nov.pdf

7. Future Expeditionary Fighting Force Needs: http://proceedings.ndia.org/4620/Chris Yunker. pdf

8. Robotics Research at the DOE - Telerobotic Controls: http://www.robotics.ost.doe.gov/reports/dd tele control fact.pdf

Section III

1. Establishing Wireless Communication via Dirigibles: http://mdI.csa.com/partners/iewrecord.php?requester=gs&collection+TRD&recid+20061050236675EA&q+uid+1023396&sctcookie+ves
2. Electronic Attack Vulnerability for Aircraft: http://stinet.dtic.mil/oaioai?&verb=getRecord& metadata Prefix=htm&identifier=ADA329367
3. An Electronic Pearl Harbor? Not Likely - Article: http://issues.org/15.1/smith.htm
4. Future ofUGVs in the Battlespace: http://www.metavr.com/technology/terrain -ugv- fcs.html
5. Interactive Robotic Control System-Teleoperated: http://wwwipr.ira.uka.de/?fileid=7

Media and Internet Articles

1. Future Fighting Wars:

   http://www.scientificamericandigital.com/index.cfm?fa-Products.ViewIssuePreview&ARTICLEIDCHAR-027AE48D-34A5-4959-BF7E-58A8D4FE259
2. US Bomber Roadmap Article: http://www. afa. org/magazine/June 1999/0699bom ber. asp
3. WikiPedia Online Future Force Entry: http://en.wikipedia.org/wiki/Future Force WarriorOnline Links to Unmanned Tech

One Links to Unmanned Tech

1. Unmanned Systems Online: http://www.auvsi.org/
2. Shepard Group Online: http://www.shephard.co. uk/UV Online/
3. Aboutcom US Military Unmanned Vehicle Article: http://usmilitary.aboutcom/cs/armyweapons/a/unmanvehicle.htm

4. Futuristic Unmanned Crusher Tele-operated Vehicle: http://www.phvsorg.com/news65 5 223 28.html
5. AUVSI http://avdil.gtri.gatech.edu/AUV S/IARCLaunchPointhtm1
6. Global Security FCS Unmanned Vehicle Overview: http://www.globalsecurity.org/military/systems/ground/fes-ugv.htm
7. Unmanned Vehicles Come of Age: DARPA Grand Challenge: http://csdl2. computer. org/comp/mags/co/2006/12/rz026. pdf
8. CRS Report to the US Congress on Unmanned Vehicles: http://www.fas.org/sgp/crs/weapons/RS21294. pdf
9. War Center 2007 Unmanned Vehicle Convention: http://www.news.navy.mil/search/display.asp?story id=26915

3

ROBOT CONTROL ARCHITECTURES FOR DEFENSE APPLICATIONS

1. Introduction

Given recent advances in robotics technologies, unmanned ground systems appear as a promising opportunity for defense applicatious. In France, teleoperated vehicles (e.g. AMX30 B2DT) will soon he used for mine breaching operations. In current advanced studies launched by the DGA (Delegation General pour l'Armement i.e. the French Defense Procurement Agency) such as PEA Mini-RoC (Programme d'Etudes Amont Mini-Robots de Choc) or PEA Demonstrateur BOA (Bul1e Operationnelle Aeroterrestre), rohotics systems are considered for military operations in urban terrain as well as in open environments, in conjunction with mounted or dismounted soldiers. To fulfil the various missions envisionned for unmanned platforms, the needs for human/robot interaction (RRI) increase so as to benefit from the orthogonal capacities of both the mall ami the machine.

In section 2, we list several missions considered for military land robots and explain related issues concerning HRI. In section 3, we present an overview of existing paradigms concerning HRI and describe a few existing applications in the field of defense robotics. In section 4, we focus on an example concerning reconnaissance missions in urban warfare and present the work on the HARPIC architecture performed at the Centre d'Expertise Parisien of the DGA. Finally, in section 5, we raise more general questions about the introduction of HRI into control architectures and about a potential standardization of these interactions, before concluding in section 6.

2. Operational Context

Missions for Military Robots

Unmanned ground systems can now be considered as key technologies for future military operations. Firstly, they remove humans from harms way by reducing their exposition on the battlefield. Moreover. they can provide various services and avoid humans dull, dirty or difficult tasks such as surveillance or heavy load carrying. More generally, in the future, they should be used as force multipliers and risk reducer in land operations.

As a result, the range of missions for unmanned ground systems in the defense and security field is widening. Among them, let us mention reconnaissance and scout missions, surveillance, target acquisition and illumination, supply delivery, mule applications, obstacle clearance, remote manipulation. Demining, explosive ordnance disposal, retrieval of injured people, communication relays, etc. These missions include different time steps from planning and deployement, mission fulfilment with human supervision and possible re-planning to reployment and maintenance as well as training sessions. They take place on various terrains, ranging from structured urban environments to destructured (destroyed) places and ill-structured or unstructured open areas. Moreover, defense operations present a few specificities compared to civil applications. Unmanned vehicles will often have to deal with challenging ill-known, unpredictable, changing and hostile environments. In urban warfare for instance, robots will face many incertainties and they will have to intermix with friends, foes and bystanders. As a partner or as an extent of a warfighter, a robot must also conform to different constraints and doctrines; he must neither increase the risk for the team—which stawls for "surprise effect" cancelling and trap triggering for instance nor impose an important workload to the human supervisor. Moreover, some decisions such as engaging a target cannot be delegated to a robot: it is crucial that man stay in the loop in such situations. Finally, robots will be inserted into large organizations (systems of systems designed for network-centric warfare and will have to co-operate with other manned or unmanned entities, following a command hierarchy. Therefore, efficient and scalable man/machine collaboration appears as a necessity.

2.2. Why introduce HRI into military operations?

On the one hand, it is desirable that robots should operate as autonomously as possible in order to reduce the workload of the operator and to be robust to communication failures with the control unit. For example, rescue operations at the World Trade Center performed using the robots developed for the DARPA (U.S. Defense Advanced Research Projects Agency) TMR (Tactical Mobile Robotics) program showed that it was difficult for a single operator to ensure both secure navigation for the robot and reliable people detection.[1]

On the other hand, technology is not mature enough to produce autonomous robots which could handle the various military situations on their own. Basic capacities that have been shown on many robots include obstacle detection awl avoiclance, waypoint and goal oriented navigation, detection of people, detection of threats, information retrieval (image, sound), localization and map building, exploration or coordination with other robots. Most of them can be implemented on a real robot with a good reliability in a reasonably difficult environment but it is not enough to fulfill military requirements. For instance, so far, no robot has been able to move fully autonomously in the most difficult and unstructured arenas of the NIST (US National Institute of Standards and Technologies) in the context of search and rescue competitions.[2] Moreover, some high-level doctrines and constraints (such as discretion) may be difficult to describe and formalize for autonomous systems.

Finally, humans and robots have complementary capabilities[3]: humans are usually superior in perception (especially in environment understanding), in knowledge management and in decision making while robots can be better than humans in quantitative low-level perception, in precise metric localization and in displacement in confined and cluttered space. Above all, robots can stand dull, dirty and dangerous jobs. Therefore, it seems that today's best solutions should rely on a good collaboration between humans and robots e.g. when robots act as antonomonsly as possible but remain under human supervision.

2.3. What kind of HRI is needed for military operations?

The modalities concerning human / robot interaction may vary development on the situation, the mission or the robotic platform. For instance, during many demining operations, the teleoperation of the robot could be performed with a direct view of the unmanned vehicle. However, the teleoperation of a tracked vehicle like the French demonstrator SYRANO (System Robotise d'Acquisition et de Neutralisation d'Objectifs) is performed with an Operator Control Unit (OCU) set up in a shelter which could be beyond line of sight if the transmission with the robot is ensured. In urban environment, the dismounted soldier in charge of the robot may need to protect himself and to operate the robot under stressful conditions either in close proximity or at a distance varying from a few meters to hundreds of meters. Concerning the effectors and the functions controlled by the human / robot team, some missions could imply precise remote manipulations with a robotic ann or the use of specific payloads (pan / tilt observation sensors, diversion equipments such as smoke-producing devices...) While others would only include effectors for the navigation of the platform. Finally, some missions may be performed in a multi-robot and multi-entities context, using either homogeneous or heteregenous vehicles, with issues ranging from authority sharing to multi-robot cooperation and insertion into network-centric warfare organizations. Therefore, defining general HRI systems for robots in defense applications may be quite challenging.

3. EXISTING HUMAN/ROBOT INTERACTION SYSTEMS

3.1. Overview of existing paradigms for HRI

Many paradigms have been developed for human robot interaction. They allow various levels of interaction with different levels of autonomy and dependance. To introduce our work concerning the HARPIC architecture as well as related work in the defense field, we attempt to briefly list below the main paradigms from the least autonomous (teleoperation) to the most advanced (mixed-initiative) where humans and robots can co-operate to determine their goals and strategies.

Teleoperation is the most basic and mature mode. In this mode the operator has full control of the robot and must assume total responsibility for mission safety and success. This mode is suitable in complicated or unexpected situations which no algorithm can deal with. In return this mode often means a heavy workload for the teleoperator who needs to focus his attention on the ongoing task. With *Supervisory control*[4] the operator (called the supervisor) orders a subordonate (the robot) to achieve a predefined plan. In this paradigm, the robot is merely a tool executing tasks under operator monitoring. This interaction mode can adapt to low level bandwith and high level control but needs constant vigilance from the operator who must react in case of failures (to perform manual mission replanning for example). This mode is only suitable for static environments where planning is really effective. *Behaviour-based teleoperation*[5] replaces fine-grained control by robot behaviours which are locally autonomous. In comparison to supervisory control, this paradigm brings safety and provides the robot with the opportunity to react to its own environment perception (e.g. to avoid obstacles). Thus, it allows the operator to be more negligent. *Adjustable autonomy*[6] refers to the adjustment of the level of autononomy which has been initiated by the operator, by another system or by the system himself and while the systern operates. The goal of this paradigm is generally to increase the negligence time allowed to the operator while maintaining the robot to an acceptable safety and effectiveness level. In *Traded control*[7] the operator controls the robot during one part of the task and the robot behaves autonomously during the other part of this task. This paradigm may lead to an equivalent of the kidnapped robot problem. While the robot is controlled by the operator, it call loose its situation awareness and face difficulties when coming back to autonomously control. In *Shared control,*[8] part of the robot functions are autonomous and the remaining are controlled by the operator. It is important to notice that this mode requires constant attention from the operator. If the robot is only in charge of some safety mechanisms, this paradigm is equivalent to the *safeguarded teleoperation. Ixed-initiative*[9] is characterized by a continuous dialogue between the operator and the robot where both of them share decision and responsibility. *Collabortive contro1*[10] may be described as a restrictive implementation of mixed-initiave. In this approach, the human robot dialogue is mainly reduced to a predefined set of questions and answers.

All this paradigms may be considered as subsets of the human / robot teaming dornain with important overlapping. Therefore, many robotic experimentation use a mix of these paradigms, including our work on HARPIC and related projects described in the next section.

3.2 Existing applications concerning defense applications

Most applications for military unmanned ground vehicles are based on existing control architectures and the HRI mechanisms often reflect this initial approach. Most of these architectures are hybrid, but some of them are more oriented towards the deliberative aspect while others focus mostly on their reactive components. As a result, HRI mechanisms are sometimes more oriented towards high level interaction at the planning phase (deliberative) while others tend to be more detailed at the reactive level.

For instance, the small UGV developed by the Swedish Royal Institute of Technology[11] for military operations in urban terrain is inspired from the SSS (Servo, Subsumption, Symbolic) hybrid architecture. The individual components correspond to reactive behaviours such as goto avoid, follow me, mapping, explore. Road-follow and inspect. During most tasks, only a single behaviour is active but when multiple behaviours are involved, a simple superposition principle is used for command fusion (following the SSS principles). The activation or desactivation of a behaviour seems to be achieved using the planning realized before the mission. The interface is stake based (modeled as a simple finite automata) so that the user can choose a task from a menu and make simple use of simple buttons to control a task. However, the authors do not describe precisely the planning module (the deliberative level) nor its relationship with the direct activation of behaviours (more reactive). Thus, it seems that the stress has been laid on the lower levels of the architecture (Servo, Subsumption).

The software architecture of the US Idaho National Engineering and Environmental Laboratory (INEEL), which has been tested by the US Space and Naval Systems Center in the scope of the DARPA TMH (Tactical Mobile Robotics) project,[12] was partially inspired by Brooks' subsumption architecture. Which provides a method for structuring reactive systems from the bottom up using layered sets of rules. Since this approach can be highly robust in unknown or dynamic environments (because it does not depend on an explicit set of actions), it has been used to create a robust routine for obstacle avoidance. Within INEEL's software control architecture. Obstacle avoidance is a bottom-up layer behaviour, and although it underlies many different reactive and deliberative capabilities, it runs independently from all other behaviours. This independence aims at reducing interference between behaviours and lowering overall complexity. INEEL also incorporated deliberative behaviours which function at a level above the reactive behaviours. Once the reactive behaviours are "satisfied", the deliberative behaviours may take control, allowing the robot to exploit a world model in order to support behaviours such as *area search, patrol perimeter* and *follow route.* These capabilities call be used in several different control modes available from INEEL's OCU (and mostly dedicated to urban terrain). In *safe mode,* the robot only takes initiative to protect itself and the environment, but allows the user to otherwise drive the robot. In *shared mode,* the robot handles the low-level navigation, but accepts intermittent input, often at the robot's request, to help guide the robot in general directions. In *autonomous mode,* the robot decides how to carry out the-Level tasks such as *follow that target* or *search this area* without any navigational input from the user. Therefore, this system call be considered as a sliding autonomy concept.

The US Army Demo III project is based on the reference architecture 4D-RCS designed by the NIST (based on the German 4D and on the NIST former RCS architectures) which allows a decomposition of the robot mission planning into numerous hierarchical levels.[13] This architecture can be considered as hybrid in the sense that it endows the robot with both reactive behaviours (in the lower levels) and advanced planning capabilities. Theoritically speaking, the operator can explicitely interact with the system at any hierarchical level. The connections to the OCU should enable a human operator to input commands, to override or modify system behaviour, to perform various types of teleoperation, to switch control modes (e.g. automatic, teleopration, siugle step, pause) and to observe the values of state variables, images, maps and entity attributes. This operator interface could also be used for programming, debugging and maintenance. However, in the scope of the Demo III program, only lower levels of the architecture have been fully implemented (servo, primitive and autonomous navigation subsystems) but they led to significant autonomous mobility capacities tested during extensive field exercises at multiple sites.[14] The OCUs feature touch screens, map-based display and context-sensitive pulldown menus and buttons. They also propose a complete set of planning tools as well as built-in mission rehearsal and simulation capabilities. In the future, the NIST awl the Demo III program managers intend to implement more tactical behaviours involving several unmanned ground vehicles, thus dressing higher levels of the 4D-RCS hierarchy. This will enable the developers to test effectively the scalability and modularity of such a hierarchical architecture.

The German demonstrator PRIMUS-D,[15] dedicated to reconnaissance in open terrain, is also compatible with the

4D/RCS achitecture. The authors provide various details about the data Hows between subsystems, which gives indications about the way HRI components could interact and be linked with robot subsystems. Within PRIUS OCU, all in-and outputs are organized in the segment "Man-Machine Interface" which enables the operator to perform mission planning, command and control of the vehicle. Inputs from the operator flow to a "coordination" segment which performs mainly plausibility checks, command anagemment and command routing.

Commands or entire mission plans are transmitted to the robot vehicle by the segment "communication", if "coordination" decides that the command could be executed by the robot. An additional software module called "payload" manages the RSTA payload. Concerning the outputs from the robot, "communications" forwards received data depending on the data type to coordination (robot state information) or to "signal and video management". On the robot side, command systems are received by a "communication" segment and forwarded to "coordination" for plausibility checks. If the command can be executed by the robot the command will be pipeline to the next segment: either "payload" if it concerns the RSTA module or "driving" and "perception" if it is related to the navigation of the platform. The PRIMUS robot can be operated according to five modes: autonomous driving with waypoint navigation, semi-autonomous driving (with high-level commands such as direction, range and velocity), remote control (assisted with obstacle detection and collision avoidance), ruml vehicle and autonomous vehicle following. It can thus be considered as an adjustable autonomy concept, including simple or behaviour- based teleoperation and autonomous modes. However, it is unclear how modular the system is and how new capabilities could be added to the system.

In the scope of the DARPA MARS (Mobile Autonomous Robotic System) program, Fong, Thorpe and Ham have developed a very rich HRI scheme based on collaborative control where humans and robots work as partners and assist each other to achieve common goals. So far, this approach has been mainly applied to robot navigation: the robot asks human questions to obtain assistance with cognition and perception during task execution. An operator profile is also defined so as to perform autonomous dialog adaptation. In this application, collaborative control has been implemented as a distributed set of modules, connected by a message-based architecture The main module of this architecture seems to be the safeguarded teleoperation controller which supports varying degrees of cooperation between the operator and the robot. Other modules include an event logger, a query manager, a user adapter, a user interface and the physical mobile robot itself.

Finally, concerning multirobot applications, the DARPA TMR program also led to the demonstration of multirobot capabilities in urban environment based on the AuRA control architecture, in relation with the MissionLab project.[16] This application relies on schema-based behavioural control (where the operator is considered as one of the available behaviours for the robots[17]) and on a usability-tested mission specification system. The software architecture includes three major subsystems: 1) a framework for designing robot missions and a means for evaluating their overall usability; 2) an executive subsystem which represents the major focus for operator interaction, providing an interface to a simulation module, to the actual robot controllers, to premission specification facilities and to the physical operator ground station; 3) a runtime control subsystem located on each active robot, which provides an execution framework for enacting reactive behaviours, acquiring sensor data, reporting back to the executive subsystem to provide situation awareness to the team commander. A typical mission starts with a planning step through the MissionLab system. This mission is compiled through a series of languages that bind it to a particular robot (Pioneer on Urbie). It is then tested in faster than real-time simulation and loaded to the real robot for execution. During execution, a console serves as monitor and control interface: it makes it possible to intervene globally on the mission execution (stop, pause, restart, step by step...), on the robot groups (using team teleautonomy, formation maintenance, bounding overwatch. By directing robots to particular regions of interest or by altering their societal personality), and on the individual robots (activating behaviours such as obstacle avoidance, waypoint following, moving towards goals, avoiding enemies, seeking hiding places, all cast into mission-spiced assemblages, using low-level software or hardware drivers such as movement commands, range measurement commands, position feedback commands, system monitoring commands, initialization and termination). The AuRA architecture used in this work can be regarded as mostly reactive: this reactivit.y appears mainly through the robot behaviours while other modules such as the permission subsystem look more deliberative (but they seem to be activated beforehand).

To conclude about these various experiences, most of these systems implement several control modes for the robot, corresponding to different autonomy levels: it seems that a single HRI mode is not sufficient for the numerous tasks and contexts military robots need to deal with. Most of them are based on well-known architectures (some of these architectures were originally designed for autonomous systems rather than semo-autonomous ones), leading to various HRI mechanisms. However, it is still difficult to compare all these approaches since we lack precise feedback (except for the few systems which were submitted to - heterogeneous but extensive performance evaluations, e.g. teleoperation /

autonomy ratio for Demo III,[18] MissionLab's usability tests[19] or urban search and rescue competitions and since they address different missions and different contexts (monorobot vs multi-robot, urban terrain vs ill-structured environments, etc.). Moreover, it is hard to assess their scalability and modularity in terms of HRI: for instance, does the addition of a new HRI mode compell the developer to modify large parts of the architecture, do they allow easy extensions to multi-robot and multi-operator conhguratious ?

In the next section, we will describe our work on the HARPIC architecture so as to illustrate and give a detailed account of an adjustable autonomy development: this description will raise more general issues about scalability and modularity, thus leading to open questions concerning the insertion of HRI within robot software architectures.

4. PRESENTATION OF OUR WORK ON HARPIC

In November 2003, the French defense procurement agency (Delegation Generally pour I' Armement) launched a prospective program called "PEA Mini-RoC" dedicated to small unmanned ground systems. This program focuses upon platform development, teleoperation and mission modules. Part of this program aims at developing autonomous functions for robot reconnaissance in urban terrain. In this context, the Centre d'Expertise Parisien (CEP) of the DGA has conducted studies to demonstrate the poteutialities of advanced control strategies for small robotic platform during military operations in urban terrain. Our goal was not to produce operational systems but to investigate several solutions on experimental platforms in order to suggest requirements and to be able to build specifications for future systems (e.g. the demonstrator for adjustable autonomy resulting from PEA TAROT).

We believe that in short term robots will not be able to handle some uncertain situations and that the most challenging task is to build a software organization which provides a pertinent and adaptive balance between robot autonomy and human control. For a good teaming, it is desirable that robots and humans share their capacities along a two-way dialogue. This is the approximate definition of the mixed-initiative control mode but, give the maturity of today's robots and the potential danger for soldiers, we do not think that Mexico-initiative could be the solution for now. Therefore adjustable autonomy, with a wide range of control modes - from basic teleoperation to even limited mixed-initiative - appears as the most pragmatic and efficient way.

Thus, based on previous work concerning our robot control architecture HARPIC, we have developed a man machine interface and software components that allow a human operator to control a robot at different levels of autonomy. In particular, this work aims at studying how a robot could be helpful in indoor reconnaissance and surveillance missions in hostile environment. In such missions, a soldier faces many threats and must protect himself while looking around and holding his weapon so that he cannot devote his attention to the teleoperation of the robot. Therefore, we have built a software that allows dynamic swapping between control modes (manual, safeguarded and behaviour-based) while automatically performing map building and localization of the robot. It also includes surveillance functions like movement detection and is designed for multirobot extensions.

We first explain the design of our agent-based robot control architecture and discuss the various ways to control and interact with a robot. The main modules and functionalities implementing those ideas in our architecture are detailed. Some experiments on a Pioneer robot equipped with various sensors are also briefly presented, as well as promising directions for the development of robots and user interfaces for hostile environment.

4.1. General Description of HARPIC

HARPIC is a hybrid architecture which consists in four blocks organized around a fifth: *perception,* an *attention manager,* a *behaviour selector* and *action processes.* The core of the architecture (the fifth block) relies on *representations.*

Sensors yield data to perception processes which create representations of the environment. Representations are instances of specialized perception models. For instance, for a visual wall-following behaviour, the representation can he restricted to the coordinates of the edge detected in the image, which stands for the wall to follow. To every representation are attached the references to the process which created it: date of creation and various data related to the sensor (position, focus...). The representations are stored with a given memory depth.

The perception processes are activated or inhibited by the attention manager and receive information on the current behaviour. This information is used to foresee and check the consistency of the representation. The attention manager has three main functions: it updates representations (on a periodical or on an exceptional basis), it supervises the environment (detection of new events) and the algorithms (prediction/feedback control), and it guarantees an efficient use of the computing resources. The action selection module chooses the robot's behaviour depending or the predefined goal(s), the current action, the representations and their estimated reliability. Finally, the behaviours control the robot's actuators in closed loop with the associated perception processes.

The key ideas of this architecture are:

- *The use of sensorimotor behaviours binding perceptions and low-level actions both internally and externally* the internal coupling allows to compare a prediction of the next perception (estimated from the previous perception and the current control) with the perception obtained after application of the control, in order to decide whether the current behaviour runs normally or should be changed; the external coupling is the classic control loop between perception and action.

- *Use of perception processes* with the aim of creating local situated representations of the environment. No global model of the environment is used; however less local and higher level representations can be built from the instantaneous local representations.
- *Quantitative assessment of every representation:* every algorithm is associated with evaluation metrics which assign to every constructed representation a numerical value expressing the confidence which can be given to it. We regard this assessment as important feature since any processing algorithm has a limited domain of validity and its internal parameters are best suited for some situations only. There is no perfect algorithm that always yields "good" results.
- *Use of an attention manager:* it supervises the execution of the perception processing algorithms independently from the current actions. It takes into account the processing time needed for each perception process, as well as the cost in terms of computational resource. It also looks for new events due to the dynamics of the environment, which may signify a new danger or opportunities leading to a change of behaviour. It may also trigger processes in order to check whether the sensors operate nominally and it can receive error signals coming from current perception processes. It is also able to invalidate representations due to malfunctioning sensors or misused processes.

- *The behaviour selection module* chooses the sensorimotor behaviours to be activated or inhibited depending on the predefined goal, the available representations and the events issued from the attention manager. This module is the highest level of the architecture. It should be noted that the quantitative assessment of the representations plays a key role in the decision process of the behaviour selection.

4.2. HARPIC implementation

Fundamental capacities of our architecture encompass modularity, encapsulation, scalability and parallel execution. To fulfill these requirements, we decided to use a multi-agent formalism which fits naturally our need for encapsulation into independent, asynchronous and heterogeneous modules. The communication between agents is realized by message. Object oriented languages are therefore absolutely suited for programming agents: we chose C++ I. We use POSIX Threads to obtain parallelism: each agent is represented by a thread in the overall process. For us, multi-agent techniques is an interesting formalism and although our architecture could be implemented without them it led to a very convenient and scalable framework.

All the agents have a common structure inherited from a basic agent and are then specialized. The basic agent can communicate by sending messages, has a mailbox where it can receive messages and runs its own process independently from other agents. Initially, all present agents have to register to a special agent called the administrator which records all information about agents (name, type, representation storage address...). All these data can be consulted by any agent. Then, when an agent is looking for another one for a specific job to do, it can access to it and to its results. It it for example what is happening when an action agent hat; to use a representation coming from a perception agent.

Perception and action agents follow the global scheme. The action agent is activated by a specific request coming from the behaviour selection agent. The selection agent order; him to work with a perception agent by sending its reference. The action agent senels in turn a request to the proper perception agent. Perception agents are passive, they only run upon request, perform a one shot execution and then wait for a new message. Furthermore, a perception agent can activate another agent and build a more specific representation using its complementary data. Many action and perception agents; run at the same time but more are waiting for messages. Only one behaviour (composed of a perception agent and an action agent) is active at the same time. Within a behaviour, it is up to the action agent to analyze representations coming from the perception agent and to establish the correct control orders for the platform.

The attention agent supervises the perception agents. It has a look-up table where it can find the types of perception agents it has to activate depending on the current behaviour. It is also in charge of checking the perception results and of declaring new events to the behaviour selection agent when necessary. The advantage of this organization is detailed in a previous paper.[21]

The selection agent has to select and activate the behaviour suited for the robot mission. This agent may be totally autonomous or constitute the process that runs the human computer interface. In this work, it is the second case and this agent is detailed in paragraph 4.4.

We use two specific agents to bind our architecture *to* hardware. The first one is an interface between the software architecture and the real robot. This agent awaits a message from an action agent before translating the instructions into comprehensible orders for the robot. Changing the real robot required; the use of a specific agent but no change in the overall architecture. The second agent acquires images from the grabber card at a regular rate and stores them in computer memory which can be consulted by perception agents.

Finally, we use a specific agent for IP communication with distant agents or other architectures. This agent has two running loops an inner loop in which it can intercept message; from other agent belonging to the same architecture, and an external loop to get data or requests; from distant architectures. This agent surpervises the (dis)appearance of distant agents or architectures. It allows the splitting of an architecture on many computers or the communication between several architectures. For example, this; agent it; useful when agent; are distributed between the robot onboard computer and the operator control unit.

4.3. Agents for SLAM and path planning

Map building is performed by a perception agent that takes laser sensor data and odometry data as input and outputs a representation which containt; a map of the environment made of registered laser scans. The map building technique used combines Kalman filtering and scan matching based on histogram correlation. This agent is executed whenever new laser data are available (e.g. 5 Hz), but it adds data to the map only when the robot has moved at least one meter since the last map update.

Localization it; performed by a perception agent that taket; odometry, laser data and the map representation as input and outputs a representation containing the current position of the robot. In its current implementation. This agent takes the position periodically estimated by the mapping algorithm and interpolates between these positions using cdometry data to provide anytime position of the robot. This agent is executed upon request by any other agent that has to use the robot position (e.g. mapping, planning, human computer interface...).

Finally, path planning is carried out by an action agent that takes the map and position representations as inputs and outputs motor commands that drive the robot toward the current goal. This agent first converts the map into an occupancy grid and using a value iteration algorithm it computes a potential that gives for every cell of the grid the length of the shortest path from this cell to the goal. The robot movements are then derived using gradient descent on this potential from the current robot position. The path planning agent is used in the *Navigation* control mode of the operator control unit (described below).

4.4. HCI agent

In this implementation, our human computer interface is a graphical interface managed by the behaviour selection agent of HARPIC. It. is designed to use a small touch-screen of 320x240 pixels such as the one that equipped most personal digital assistant (PDA). With this interface, the user has to select a screen corresponding to one of the control mode he want to activate or a screen showing the environment measures and representations built, by the robot. These screens are described below.

The *Teleop* screen corresponds to a teleoperation mode where the operator controls the translational and the rotational speed of the robot by defining on the screen the end of the speed vector. The free space measured by the laserscanner can be superimposed on the screen and it appears in white color. The operator can also activate anti-collision and obstacle avoidance functions. Messages announcing obstacles are also displayed. This screen allows full teleoperation of the robot displacement (with or without seeing it thanks to the laser free space representation) as well as safeguarded teleoperation. As a result the operator has full control on the robot in order to trade with precise movement in cluttered space or with autonomous mobility failure. In return, he must keep defining the robot speed vector otherwise it stops and waits. A functionnality related to the reflexive teleoperation[12] concept also enables the operator to activate behaviours depending on the events detected by robot. Indeed, clicking on "wall" or "corridor" messages appearing on the screen makes the system trigger "wall following" or "corridor following" behaviours, thus activating a new control mode.

The *Image* screen allows to control the robot by pointing at a location or defining a direction within the image acquired by the onboard robot camera. As the previous mode, this one enables full control or safeguarded teleoperation for the robot displacement. Two sliders operate the pan and tilt unit of the camera. When the *Go To XY* function is enabled, the location selected by the operator in the image is translated into a robot displacement vector by projection onto the ground plane with respect to the camera calibration and orientation angles. The *Direction* function moves the robot when the operator defines the end of the speed vector on the screen. The selectable *Laser* function draws a polygonal view of the free space in front of the robot (in an augmented reality way) which is built from the projection of the laser range data in the image. This "Tron-like" representation allows to control the robot in the image whenever there is no sufficient light for the camera. Incidentally, this function provides a visual checking of the good correspondance between the laser data and the camera data. If the Go *To XY* or *Direction* functions are not enabled and if the robot is in any autonomous mode, this screen can be used by a operator to supervise the robot action by viewing the images of the onboard camera. However, it can stop the robot in case of emergency.

The *Navigation* screen shows a map of the area already explored by the robot. In this control mode, the operator has to point out at a goal location in the map to trigger an autonomous displacement of the robot up to this goal. The location can be changed dynamically (whenever the previous goal has not been reached). The planning process is immediate (a few seconds). When new areas are discovered the map is automatically updated. The map is an occupancy grid where bright areas correspond to location which have been observed as free more often than darkest area. Three sliders can translate or zoom the displayed map. This is an autonomous control mode where the operator can select a goal and forget the robot.

The *Agents* screen allows the composition and the activation of behaviours by selecting an appropriate pair of perception and action agents. For example, it allows to execute behaviours like obstacle avoidance, wall following or corridor following with different perception or action agents (each one corresponding to a specific sensor or algorithm) for a same behaviour. For example, a wall following behaviour can result from a perception agent using the camera, from another one using the laser scanner and from various algorithms. This control mode corresponds to the behaviour based teleoperation paradigm. However, this screen has been mainly designed for expert users awl development purpose. It lacks simplicity but it will be easily reduced to a shall number of buttons when the most effective behaviours set will be determined.

The *Prog* screen corresponds to predefined sequences of behaviours. For example, it enables the robot to alternate obstacle avoidance and wall or corridor following when respectively an obstacle, a wall or a corridor appears in the robot trajectory. This example is a kind of sophisticated wander mode. More generally, this mode allows antonyms tasks that could he described as a sequence of behaviours like exploration or surveillance where observation and navigation behaviours are combined. The list of these sequences can he easily angmented to adapt the robot to a particular mission. In this control mode, the robot is autonomous and the operator workload could be null.

A *MultiRobot* screen allows the operator to select the robot which will be controlled by his control unit. Indeed, our interface and software architecture is designed to address more than one robot. In a platoon with many robots this capacity may give way to the sharing of each robot data or representation and to the exchange of robot control between soldiers.

The *Local Map* and *Global Map* screens show the results of the SLAM agents described in 4.3. The first one is a view of the free zone determined on each laser scan. The second one displays the global map of the area explored by the robot and its trajectory. The circle on the trajectory indicates the location where the SLAM algorithm has added new data. The current position of the robot is also shown on the map. As on some others screens, sliders allow the operator to translate and to zom the display. These screens may be used when the robot is in any autonomous mode to supervise its movements.

The *Detection* screen displays moving objects trajectory in the map built by the robot. This screen stands for surveillance purpose. The algorithm used is based on movement detection on laser range data and Kalman filtering. This screen shows that this interface is not limited to displacement control of the robot but is able to be extended to many surveillance tasks.

The transition between any autonomous or teleoperation screens causes the ending of the current action or behaviour. These transitions have been designed to appear natural to the operator. However, when one of these modes is actived, it is still possible to use the screens that display robot sensors data or representations without disactivating them. This feature is valid for the operator control unit but also for other control units. Thus, in a soldier team images and representations from a given robot can be viewed by a team member that is not responsible for the robot operation.

4.5. Experimentation

The robot we used both in indoor and outdoor experiments is a Pioneer 2AT from Active-Media equipped with sonar range sensors, color camera (with motorized lens and pan-tilt unit) and an IBEO laser range sensor. On board processing is done by a rugged Getac laptop running Linux and equipped with IEEE802. wireless link, frame grabber card and Arcnet card for connection to the laster. We also use another laptop with the same wireless link that plays the role of the operator control unit. The agents of the robot control architecture are distributed on both laptops. We did not use any specialized hardware or real-time operating system.

Several experiments have been conducted in the rooms and corridors of our building and have yielded good results. In such an environment with long linear walls or corridors, the automous displacement of the robot using the implemented behaviours is effective. However, in this particular space, a few limitations for the SLAM process have been identified. They mainly come from the laser measurement when the ground plane hypothesis is not valid and in the presence of glass surfaces.

The largest space we have experimented so far was the exhibition hall of the JNRR'03 conference.[23] It took place in the machine-tool hall of the Institute Francais de Mecanique Avancee (IFMA) and in the presence of many visitors. These moving objects introduced some sparse and isolated edges on the map but did not disturb the map building process. The robot travelled an area about 60×60m large with loops and abrupt heading changes. The robot displacement was mainly done in the safeguarded teleoperation mode because the building lacked main structures and directions for the robot to follow and because of the presence of people.

These experiments have revealed some missing functions in our interface (e.g. in mission map initialization, manual limitation of the space map, goto starting point behaviour...) but no deep change requirement in the software architecture have been discovered.

4.6. Future Work

Our human computer interface runs on a PC laptop with Linux and Qt C++ toolkit for the graphic interface. It is currently being implemented on a PDA with Linux and Qtopia environment. Moreover, new functions and behaviours are being integrated onto the platform such as exploration, go-back-home and assistance in narrow space crossing like doors. More mission-oriented behaviours such as surveillance and people or vehicle recognition would also enhance our system and make it more directly suited to operational contexts. In the meantime, we keep improving existing behaviours to make them as robust as possible. Development of extended multi-robot capacities, interaction and cooperation are also planned as a second step.

Concerning HRI, beyond considerations about ergonomy and usability of the interface, we consider working on semi-autonomous transition mechanisms between the various control modes, thus extending the simple reflexive teleoperation functionnalities described above. These transitions could be triggered by changes in the environment complexity for instance: knowing the validity domain of the behaviours, it seems possible to activate more adapted behaviours, to suggest a switch towards another mode[24] or to request the help of the human operator. This would also lead to more sophisticated interaction modes such as cooperative control. On-line evaluation of the overall performance of behaviours or autonomy modes[24] also appears as a promising direction, all the more so as such evaluation mechanisms are already integrated within our architectures.

Finally, it could he interesting to introduce more direct human/robot interactions for the various kinds of agents (beyond the interface agent). Perception agents might benefit from human cognition in order to confirm object identification for instance. Action agents might request human assistance when the robot cannot deal autonomously with challenging environments, while the attention agent could he interested by new human detected events which would warn the robot about potential dangers or opportunities.

5. Perspectives and Open Issues

The various HRI mechanisms existing in the literature, including our work on HARPIC, raise many general questions. For instance, generally speaking, how can we modify existing control architectures so as to introduce efficient HRI ? What features would make some architectures more adapted to HRI than others? What kind of HRI is supported by existing architectures? Is it possible to conceive general standard architectures allowing any kind of HRI ? What about scalability and modularity for HRI mechanisms? Which HRI modalities can be considered as most efficient within defense robotics applications? All these questions can still be considered as open issues. However, based on the examples described in the previous sections and on the recent advances in software technologies, we can provide a few clues concerning these topics.

5.1. HRI within a robot control architecture

5.1.1. HRI modes

Humans and robots have different perception, decision and action abilities. Therefore, it is crucial that they should help each other in a complementary way. Depending on the autonomy control mode, the respective roles of the man and the robot may vary (see[26] for instance for a description of these roles according to the control mode). However, in existing interaction models, humans define the high-level strategies which are almost lever transmitted to the robot: in the most advanced cases, the robot only knows task schedules or behaviours he must execute.

We have already described eight different HRI modes in section 3.1. Some variants such as safeguarded teleoperation or reflexive teleoperation could also be mentioned. Moreover, other approaches have been proposed to characterize autonomy e.g., ALFUS[27] or ANS,[28] which could lead to other HRI mode definitions.

In the context of military applications, we have seen that adjustable antonomy can be considered as a promising mode. However, adjustable autonomy can lead to various mechanisms concerning control mode definitions and transition mechanism between modes: these complicated issues are currently being addressed in the scope of PEA TAROT (Technologies d'Autonomie decisionnelle pour la Robotique Terrestre) for example.

5.1.2. Functions and functional levels concerned by HRI

Any function of the robot may be concerned by HRI, whether it be perception, decision or action. In any architecture a human robot interface can theoretically replace any component receiving information and sending commands. However, in many cases, it is not meaningful to make such a replacement since some of these components can be dealt with (automated or computed) by machines very effectively. Indeed, the control of a mobile robot can globally operate at three different functional levels. At the lower level, it represents a direct control on effectors with sensory feedback and/or a direct view on the robot (teleoperation). At the next level, the operator is in charge of the selection of tasks or behaviours. The upper level corresponds to the supervision where the operator takes part in the mission planning; and monitors its execution. Depending on the design approach (respectively reactive, behavioural or deliberative), a control architecture can be modified in order to integrate a specific HRI operating either on the actuator commands, on the behaviours or on the mission planning/execution. This order might be difficult to bypass. For instance, on a very deliberative architecture including a planning module dedicated to the robot management, it would not be desirable that a HRI could enable an operator to intervene at the actuator or the behaviour level (if the latter exists). Indeed, it might seriously disturb the planning execution (leading to the kidnapped robot syndrom).

Thus, within some architectures, interaction with other agents is only allowed at the highest levels. For instance, an extension of the three-tier architecture to the RETSINA MAS[2] only plans communications with the high-level reasoning layer. In specific contexts such as HRI in close proximity, the LAAS is currently developing sophisticated and dedicated interaction mechanisms (based on common human/robot goals) within the decisional layer of its architecture.[29] In DORO control architecture the user can interact with the higher module (the executive layer) during the planning phase (posting new goals, modifying planning parameters or the generated plan, etc.) And with the middle functional layer during the executive phase (e.g. deciding where the rover has to go or when some activities should stop). Nevertheless, the operator is not supposed to communicate with the lower physical layer. On the other hand, in simple reactive architectures like DAMN, command arbitration allows behaviours as diverse as human teleoperation and robot autonomous safety modules to co-exist.[31] Finally in a hybrid architecture such as Harpic, where behaviour chaining or planning are only considered as an advice, there is no major obstacle to the introduction (or the modification) of an HRI at any functional level. In general hierarchical architectures like NASREM,[32] 4D/RCS[13] or 3T,[6] HRI is also planned at every level so that autonomous behaviours can possibly override human commands or conversely be interrupted through human interventions.

Moreover, we can notice that hybrid architectures seem well adapted to the insertion of HRI thanks to the concept of sensorimotor behaviours, which are usually quite meaningful for humans. These behaviours also look like the "elementary actions" of the soldiers, which also makes them good candidates for defense applications.

5.1.3. Human / Robot interfaces

Human / Robot interfaces are key components of semiautonomous robots and they can be considered as part of their architecture. Roughly speaking, interfaces must provide the operator with information (or raw measurements) collected by the robot sensors and allow him to send orders. The semantic level of information and commands may vary but today, they are still inferior to those currently manipulated by humans. The interface can however display global and high-level information built by other human actors (such as the tactical situation). More details can be found in[26] for instance concerning classical basic and additional services for human / robot interfaces.

5.2. Constraints and limitations for the HRI design

5.2.1. Security constraints

In any given architecture, it seems possible (and sometimes necessary) to replace. double or duplicate a component (receiving information and sending commands) by a human/robot interface in the case when the human operator expertise or responsibility is not possible to avoid, for instance to ensure people and goods security. For instance, a robot must not endanger people in its vicinity.

5.2.2. Technical constraints about communication bandwidth and real time

Every functional level can be associated with a frequency concerning order exchange and information feedback between the human operator and the robot, especially within dynamic environments. For instance, to control an actuator level using a video feedback, the communication flow between the human and the robot must be important and very steady. On the other hand, a control at the mission planning level can accomodate sparse and even irregular communications with low bandwidth. The choice of the software and hardware communication technologies between the interface and the command receiver/information provider systems will depend on this constraint.

5.2.3. Constraints concerning ergonomics and human capacities

In the multirobot case or more generally when robots outnumber humans, it is not conceivable that robots should only be controlled at the actuator level since human operators will suffer from a heavy workload. Higher level commands (at the behaviour or mission levels) are necessary. Moreover, it might be useful to reduce (filter) the information provided to the interfaces (e.g. within limited reality concepts) and to endow robots with autonomous behaviours so that they can carry on the mission on their own when they have not received any order.

The notion of user profile could be also used to adapt the content of an interface as well as its level of control so that it becomes better suited to a given human operator.[10] This process may refer to adaptation to the operator preferences, capacities or states (using pulse monitoring, temperature...).

The interface should also adapt to the environment, e.g. by simplifying displays, showing only the most important information in emergency situations or selecting the information depending on the context.

5.2.4. Hardware constraints

At the hardware level, a human/robot interface is made both of an information output and order input device. The standardization constraint of an interface will mainly lie in the fact that one must avoid to use devices whose integration and ergonomy have not been specifically designed and adapted to a particular application such as a pilot joystick containing all degrees of freedom and buttons corresponding to the robot functions. In the near future, the most standard interface will probably composed of a keyboard and a screen (tactile screen) or possibly a simple joystick. A specific interface can be simulated by a standard one (i.e. a tactile screen), despite a reduced ergonomy and probably a decreasing efficacity of the operator when sending orders.

5.2.5. HRI dependence from missions, platforms, payloads and interface devices

Concerning general HRI modes, independence seems quite challenging since context may induce very different HRI needs. For instance, dismounted soldiers will probably not be able to bear as much workload as mounted soldiers sheltered in an armoured control unit. They may also operate in close vicinity with the robot which will lead to specific collaboration schemes due to security reasons for instance (which might be similar to service robotics approaches) while remote operation of robot will imply other relationships with the robot, with awareness problems similar to those encountered urban search and rescue (USAR) challenges.

Each mission and each environment can be associated to specific platform, payload and HRI device categories. In a dynamic and hostile environment, a dismounted soldier should use a simple, intuitive and small interface, which will be quite different from the one used by his unit commander in his command and control shelter. However, all these equipments can be built based on the same software technologies and on common communication interfaces.

5.3. New software technologies for HRI

Like usual systems in everyday life, military systems are evolving from very centralized computing towards distributed computing. Future warriors will be equiped with numerous sensors, will wear "smart" clothes and will team with various semi-autonomous systems. They will rely on technologies such as "ubiquitous, ambient and pervasive computing". Well-accepted and efficient computing needs to be context-sensitive, taking into account individual, collective as well as social dimensions.

Generally speaking (beyond robotic applications), multi-agent systems (MAS) enable coordination between distributed operations, creation of open systems with increasing complexity and increasing abstraction levels. This paradigm was developed around notions such as autonomy, interaction, organization and emergence to emphasize the relationship between the user and the system. Practically speaking, MAS combine several emerging technologies: distributed computing such as "grid-computing" (investigating how to use distributed and dynamically accessible computing resources in an efficient way), artificial intelligence, constrained programming, learning, data mining, planning, scheduling and web semantics. Thus, MAS make it possible to move from a traditional, centralized, closed and passive structure to a decentralized, open and pro-active conception. They are characterized by notions such as extensibility, portability, robustness, fault or failure tolerance and reliability.

Real-time issues as well as complex, conistrained and embedded systems are still not fully adressed in the MAS commnnity. However, agents can be created to adders specific capabilities. Concerning real-time issues, numerous studies propose anytime algorithms providing results which are all the more satisfying as the algorithm execution time increases. These algorithms can be interrupted anytime, the quality of the result depending on the time allocated to their execution. Within HARPIC, this capability has been implemented using several agents dedicated to the same task, corresponding to algorithms with different costs. The selection of a specific agent thus depends on the available computing time and on its cost.[25]

As a result, it seems that the numerous capacities and technologies involved in MAS are well suited to new operational concepts such as network-centric warfare, where human and manned systems are supposed to interact with semiautonomous and robotic entities. The multi-agent paradigm also appears as an interesting framework for the development of robot control architectures designed for defense applications. Indeed, multi-agent systems enable to build bottom-up applications, without being contained with evolving technical requirements. The conception of military systems (or systems of systems) whose life cycle may turn out to be long could thus benefit from the multi-agent paradigm. Indeed, agents can be considered as services which can be used by the system depending on its current needs.

Multi-threading and object-oriented languages can also facilitate the development of software architecture for robots. Especially in a multi-agent framework. Beyond the similarity between the object and the agent concepts the object-oriented language C++ has allowed us to develop common structures for agent hierarchies, inheriting from mechanisms such as communication by messages between the agents. For example without resorting to multi-agent systems, the conceptors of the CLARAty architecture (considered as NASA future architecture) have also opted for an object-oriented approach in order to facilitate code rensability and extension Indeed, this approach favors a hierarchical an modular decomposition of the system at different levels of abstraction. For instance, a class can provide a locomotion function which will be more and more specialized as it comes closer to the effectors (wheels, tracks...). This approach could also favor a hierarchical decomposition of the HRI, depending on the precision of the information or orders exchanged between both entities.

As for most parts of the software architecture, the development of HRI mechanisms will probably rely on various tools and tool sets. These tools are likely to be unified within integration platforms including both architecture and environment and containing all the necessary functionalists to create interfaces and interaction modes, ranging from specification. He assistance to simulation and validation tools (see[16] for instance).

5.4. HRI scalability

Scalability can be viewed as an extension capability avoiding:

- extensive studies concerning the design of the architecture when adding new functionalists;
- incompatibilities, disturbances or dead-lock between system components;
- reduced performances which could be due to coordination issues between the system components or to communication bottlenecks.

To tackle (and possibly solve) this problem, military organizations rely on specialized yet adaptive unities for every activity (based on human adaptation capabilities), communication and local negociation or re-organization capabilities for every component, as well as a strong hierarchy wherein orders and reports flow rapidly.

Specialization, communication and hierarchy are quite easy to reproduce on software systems. Adaptation (including learning). Negotiation and re-organization remain more open issues. Some of these capabilities have been developed for communication purposes for example. Where QOS (quality of service) or transmission handwidth are negociated depending on the quality of the medium. They are also at the core of an emblematic advanced project by IBM concerning "Autonomic Computing", where a MAS-based system aims at delegating to software systems part of their own management, using self-healing and self-analysing agents. Moreover, agent hierarchization and priorizing mechanisms have already been implemented on MAS. which appear as a promising paradigm in terms of adaptation, negociation and re-organization. Indeed, such capabilities are part of the motivations for creating MAS.

Concerning the information or the representations which are to be manipulated within future large systems and systems of systems (containing both humans and robots), it seems difficult today to plan everything in advance. It should be possible to define the detail level for every entity. The information which could be delivered by entities of higher, similar or lower hierarchical ranks should be submitted to queries and answers, according to context-dependent rules or hierarchical decisions. One could thus envision future military network-centric systems as some kinds of web-services endowed with hierachical rights and improved security.

5.5. HRI standardization

Current design approaches concerning robot software architectures may not exploit the full possibilities for HRI (e.g. a given architecture may not adapt to any HRI mode):

the emergence of reference and standardized architectures might help to reduce these specificities. Moreover, standards for architectures and for associated HRI would probably facilitate the extension of current systems, the specification and development of new architectures as well as the validation of their design.

However, HR.I standardization goes beyond the simple fact of using standard technologies. It requires modular conception and component scalability as well. Thus, important issues remain reganling HBI design. Is it possible to build generic logical views of control architecture with associated HRI components, including the communication mechanisms between these components? Is there a limitation in this standardization taking into account the wide range of missions for robots or the various HRI modes?

Concerning the specific components that should appear in generic logical views of architectures including HRI, it seems that depending on the approach, new components may arise. For instance, in the context of service robotics, LAAS has defined interaction agents (representing interacting humans at the robot decisional level) as well as task delegates (monitoring task execution towards the goal and the level of engagement of interaction agents through specific observers)[29] In the case of Fong's approach about collaborative control,[3] specific segments have also been added such as a query manager or a user adapter. The challenge would thus consist in building views which would remain general enough to avoid specific solutions (related to specific contexts) and at the same time that would remain detailed enough so as to be useful during the specification, development and validation phases of new architectures.

At the software level, the standardization of human / robot interfaces including communication with surrounding systems is not very different from the standardization of any human/machine interface communicating with a wider application: this subject has been extensively studied in the field of distributed computing. For instance, the 3-tier architecture aims at dividing an application into three layers: a presentation layer, a processing layer and a data access layer. The presentation layer, i.e. the display and the dialog with the user can be based on HTML (using a web navigator) or on WML (using a GSM). Architectures such as SOAP (service oriented architectures), which have become popular through Web-services, make it possible to create services (software components with a strong inner coherence) with weak external coupling. These architectures rely on standards such as XML (Extensible Markup Language) for data description, WSDL (Web Services Description Language) for the description of service interfaces, UDDI (Universal Description Discovery and Integration) for service index management and SOAP (Simple Object Access Protocol) for service calling.

In military information systems, standards (16 or 22 links, MIDS...) have already been developed to exchange numerical messages, concerning tactical situations for instance. In MAS, interaction languages between agents have been specified within the multi-agent community, e.g. KQML or ACL (Agent Communication Language) from the FIPA (Foundation for Intelligent Physical Agents).

These technologies and the associated mechanisms could be used for software standardization purposes, for instance within networks where robots would interact with human operators and various other systems. It seems that these standards could also be considered as references for future HRI purposes in the defense field.

For example, in a very prospective approach, similarly to common approaches used in the web-services, could it be interesting to integrate a service index at the battlefield network level, allowing the negotiation of services between all entities? Will we see robots and soldiers naturally sharing information, helping each other to do their job and fulfill their mission?

6.Conclusion

In this article, we first listed some operational missions which could involve unmanned vehicles and explained various needs for HRI. In the next section, we mentioned a few robotic systems designed for military applications and described the HRI component within their software architectures. Then we presented our work concerning the development of an effective software enabling to control a reconnaissance robot: we have created a robot control architecture based on a multi-agent paradigm which allows various levels of autonomy and interaction between an operator and the robot. According to the state of the art in robot autonomy in hostile environment we think that *adjustable autonomy* is one of the most pertinent choice for the next generation of military robots. Our work shows that many control modes with seamless transitions can be fairly integrated in a quite simple operator control unit. It has also confirmed the good behaviour of our software architecture HARPIC and the great advantage of the flexible multi-agent approach when adding many functions. Moreover, this kind of interface is a good mean to experiment, evaluate or demonstrate autonomous robot behaviours and HRI, which will hopefully allow us to gather more military requirements and to improve the specification of future systems. Finally, based on the lessons learned from the development of this software architecture and from other related work, we discussed more general issues concerning the adaptation of existing architectures to HRI and the possible standardization of HRI within reference architectures. We also proposed a few guidelines for the practical development of softwares for architectures which would be suited to HRI.

To conclude military contexts offer a wide rnage of situations for robots and tackling these issues could lead to numerous innovations in the field of HRI. Even though some of these problems are currently addressed in prospective programs launched by the DGA such as PEA Mini-RoC, PEA TAROT or PEA Demonstrateur BOA, there is still a major effort to be done in order to meet tomorrow needs,

Acknowledgments

The work concerning HARPIC was entirely performed within the Geomatics-Imagery-Perception department of the Centre d'Expertise Parisien of the DGA. The authors would like to thank S. Moudere, E. Sellami, N. Sinegre, F. Souvestre, D. Lucas, R. Cornet, G. Calba, C. Couprie and R. Cuisinier for their contributions to the software development of this work. They are also very grateful to D. Filliat, M. Lambert, E. Moline and D. Luzeaux who shared their reflexions about autonomy and human/robot interaction and helped to improve the HARPIC system.

REFERENCES

1. S. Pratt, T. Frost., A. M. Shein, C. Norman, M. Ciholas, G. More, and C. Smith, "Applications of TMR technology to urban search and rescue: lessons learned at the WTC (disaster," iu *SPIE AeroSense, Unmanned Ground Vehicle Technology IV*, (Orlando, USA), 2002.
2. 1. R. Nourbakhsh, K. Sycara. M. Koes, M. Yong, M. Lewis, and S. Burion, "Human-robot teaming for search and rescue," in *Pervasive Computing,* 2005.
3. T. Fong, C. Thorpe, and C. Baur, "Collaboration, dialogue. and humau-robot interaction," in *Proceedings of the 10th International Symposium of Robotics Research,* (Lome (Victoria, Australia)), November :2001.
4. P. Backes, K. Tso, and G. Tharp, "The web interface for telescience," in *IEEE International Conference on Robotics and Automation, ICRA* '97, (Albuquerque, NM), 1997.

5. M. Stein, "Behaviour-based control for time-delayed teleoperation," Tech. Rep. 378, GRASP Laboratory, University of Pennsylvania, 1994.
6. G. Dorais, R. Bonasso, D. Kortenkamp, B. Pell, and D. Schreckenghost, "Adjustable autonomy for human centered autonomous systems on Mars.," in *6th International Joint Conference on Artificial Intelligence (IJCAI), Workshop on Adjustable Autonomy System,* 1999.
7. D. Kortenkamp, R. Bonasso, D. Ryan, and D. Schreckenghost, "Traded control with autonomous robot as mixed initiative interaction," in *14th National Conference on Artificial Intelligence,* (Rhode Island, USA), july 1997.
8. T. Rofer and A. Lankenau, "Ensuring safe obstacle avoidance in a shared-control system," in *Seventh International Conference on Emergent Technologies and Factory Automation, EFTA*'99, (Barcelonna, Spain), 1999.
9. G. Ferguson, J. Allen, and B. Miller, "TRAINS-95: Towards a mixed-initiative planllillg assistant," in *Third International Conference on AI Planning Systems, AIPS-96,* 1996.
10. T. Fong, C. Thorpe., and C. Baur, "Collaborative contro1: a robot-centered model for vehicle teleoperation," *in AAAI Spring Symposium on Agents with Ajustable Autonomy, Technical report SS-99-06,* (Memlo Park), 1999.
11. H.I. Christensen, J. Folkesson, A. Hedstr'o, and C. Lundberg, "UGV technology for urban navigation," in *SPIE Defense and Security Conference, Unmanned Ground Vehicle Technology VI,* (Orlando, USA), 2004.
12. E. B. Pacis, H. R. Everett, N. Farrington, and D. Bruemmer, "Enhancing functionnality and autonomy in man-portable robots," in *SPIE Defence and Security Conference, Unmanned Ground Vehicle Technology VI,* (Orlando. USA), 2004.
13. J. Albus, "4D IRCS: a reference model architecture for intelligent unmanned ground vehicles," in *SPIE AeroSense Conference, Unmanned Ground Vehicle Technology IV,* (Orlando, USA), 2002.
14. J. A. Bornstein. "Army ground robotics research program," in *SPIE AeroSense Conference, Unmanned Ground Vehicle Technology IV,* (Orlando, USA), 2002,

15. G. Schaub, A. Pfaendner, and C. Schaefer, "PRIMUS" autonomous navigation in open terrain with a tracked vehicle." in *SPIE Defense and Security Conference, Unmanned Ground Vehicle Technology VI,* (Orlando. USA), 2004.
16. R. C. Arkin, T. R. Collins, and Y. Endo, "Tactical mobile Robot mission specification and execution," in *Mobile Robots* XIV, pp.50-63, (Boston, MA), September 1999.
17. K.S. Ali and R.C. Arkin, "Multiagent teleautonomous behavioural control," in *Machine Intelligence and Robotic Control (IROC).* 1(1), pp.3-17, 2000.
18. B.A. Bodt and R.S. Camden, "Technology readiness level 6 and autonoous mobility," in *SPIE AeroSense Conference, Unmanned Ground Vehicle Technology VI,* (Orlando, USA), April 2004.
19. Y. Endo, D. C. MacKenzie, and R. C. Arkin, "Usability evaluation of high-level user assistance for robot mission specification," *in Special Issues on Human-Robot Interaction of the SMC Transactions: Part* C,2004.
20. J. Scholtz, B. Antonishek, and J. Young, "Evaluation of human-robot interaction in the NIST reference search and rescue test arenas," in *Performance Metrics for Intelligent Systems (PerMIS'04),* 2004.
21. D. Luzeaux and A. Dalgalarrondo, *Hybrid architecture based on representations. perception and intelligent control,* ch. Studies in Fuziness and Soft Computing: Recent Advances in Intelligent Paradigms and Applications. ISBN-3-7908-1538-1, Physica Verlag, Heildelberg, 2003.
22. T. Rofer, "Using histogram correlation to create consistent laser scan maps," in *IEEE International Conference on Robotics Systems (IROS-2002),* (EPFL, Lausanne. Switzerland), 2002.
23. "Quatriemes Journees Nationales de Recherche en Robotique (JNRR'03)," (Clennont-Ferrand, France, http://lasmea, univ-bpclermont.fr/jurr03/), 8-10 October 2003.
24. M. Baker and H. A. Yanco, "Autonomy mode suggestions for improving human-robot interaction," in *IEEE Conference on Systems, Man and Cyberndics,* October 2004.

25. A. Dalgalarronrlo, *Integration de la function perception dans une architecture de controle de robot mobile autonome.* PhD thesis, Universite de Paris-Sud, Centre d'Orsay, janvier 2001.

26. A. Dalgalarrondo, "De l'autonomie des systemes robotises," in *Technical report,* n'f. *CTA/02 350 180/RIEX/807,*2003.

27. H.-M. Huang, K. Pavek, J. Albus, and E. Messina, "Autonomy levels for unmanned systems (ALFUS) framework: An update," in *SPIE Defence and Security Conference, Unmanned Ground Vehicle Technology VII,* (Orlawlo, USA), 200.5.

28. G. M. Kamsickas and J. N. Ward, "Developing UGVS for the FCS program," in *SPIE AeroSense, Unmanned Ground Vehicle Technology V,* (Orlando, USA), 2003.

29. R. Alami, A. Clothe, V. Montreuil, E. A. Sishot, and R. Chatila, "Task planning for human-rohot interaction." in *Joint sOc-EUSAI conference,* October 200.5.

30. A. Finzi and A. Orlandini, "A mixed-initiative approach to human-robot interaction in rescue scenarios," in *International Conference on Automated Planning and Scheduling (ICAPS), Printed Notes of Workshop on Mixed-Initiative Planning and Scheduling,* pp. 36-43, 2005.

31. T. Fong, C. Thorpe, awl C. Baur, "Multi-robot remote (lriving with collaborative control," in *IEEE Transactions on Industrial Electronics,* 50(4), August 2003.

32. J. Albus, R. Lumia, J. Fiala, and A. Wavering, "NASREM: the NASA/NBS standard reference model for telerobot control system architecture," in *Technical report, Robot System Division, National Institute of Standards and Technology,* 1987.

33. F. Ingrand. "Architectures logicielles pour la robotique autonome," in *Quatriemes Journees Nationales de Recherche en Robotique* (JNRR'03), (Clermmont-Ferrand, France), October 2003.

4

ROBOTIC TRENDS

> *World events and the military seem to have rendered moot the first of three Rules of Robotics laid down in Isaac Asimov's sci-fi classic I, Robot, namely "A robot must never harm a human being, or through inaction, allow a human being to come to harm."*
>
> *by Ed Moser*

The mountains of broken steel, shattered concrete and superheated rubble left at the World Trade Towers site in the aftermath of the events of September 11, 2001, made it impossible for human rescuers to sift through the ruins in search of bodies and possible survivors. So officials at the site turned to mechanical alternatives - a collection of 17 treaded, basketball-sized machines. They had been developed through the Defense Department's five-year, $50 million Tactical Mobile Robots (TMR) Program. Over 11 days the robots crawled about the tiny, hellish voids of Ground Zero, and discovered seven bodies. At the same time, another group of three small robots from the University of South Florida clambered over the same terrain. They pointed cameras to distinguish splotches of blood from the gray dust that smothered the debris, and carried microphones to listen for cries for help.

By the following summer, variants of the mechanical rescuers were helping wreak revenge on the collaborators of the 9/11 attacks. The Pentagon had asked iRobot, a MIT spin-off, to retool its Packbot robot for military duty. In one month of service in Afghanistan, the 42-pound, rubber treaded robots, with Pentium 3 processor brains, assisted in clearing out three buildings, three bunkers, and two-dozen caves. Wide-angle and zoom cameras perched above the squat bodies of the robots enabled soldiers to safely inspect the interiors of buildings in real time. Engineers rigged a network of repeaters to let the $40,000 contrivances radio back signals from within deep caverns. Global Positioning Satellite (GPS) technology and digital compasses kept the Packbots properly oriented.

After Afghanistan came Iraq, and further successes by land robots and air-borne robot drones. "Robots," noted the National Academy of Sciences (NAS) in a 2002 report on Army unmanned vehicles, "are fearless and tireless. They do repetitive tasks with speed and precision."

The Pentagon is now pouring money into "bots," making military robotics a new growth industry. For fiscal years 2004-2009, the Army is allocating $500 million to unmanned ground platforms. On a similar note, the Defense Advanced Research Projects Agency (DARPA) is bankrolling over 40 robot-related projects in universities and in private firms.

Robots for the Ground Forces

The military's plans for land-based robots are extremely ambitious. If put into practice over the next two decades, they would revolutionize the current array of ground weapons, replacing today's Abram's tanks and Bradley

Fighting Vehicles with swarms of unmanned, autonomous vehicles bristling with missiles and long-range guns, and sewn together with multi-frequency wireless networks. Some critics are skeptical that the proposed deployment time frame to supplement or supplant mechanized ground troops with ground-based mobile robots is sufficient to overcome the daunting technical hurdles associated with the endeavour. But even if that heady vision remains unrealized, robots will likely become a major component of the armed forces' standard land arsenal by 2010.

The blueprint for the Army's transformation is its Future Combat System (FCS). Under the FCS, three major groups of robots are envisioned for the wars of the 21 st century: a portable reconnaissance robot, a medium-sized transport and recon vehicle, and a large fighting platform. Their roles would be to search out and identify enemy forces and call in strikes from unmanned, autonomous land vehicles and pilotless aircraft. DARPA and the Army have selected United Defense, the Manned Ground Vehicle design team of Being and Science Applications International Corporation (SAIC), and General Dynamics Land Systems, as the major FCS contractors for the construction of eight different land vehicles.

The FCS is in its early design stages, and could undergo significant changes. An Army task force has reported that it may be 2025 before fully autonomous ground vehicles are fielded.

Small Unmanned Ground Vehicles

The first Future Combat System vehicle type, the Small Unmanned Ground Vehicle (SUGV), will be outfitted with sensors for reconnaissance. The 30-pound SUGV is envisioned to be light enough for a single soldier to transport, and nimble enough to climb up stairs and move through rubble. SUGVs could also be equipped with communication sensors and grenades. They will be cheap enough, about $30,000 each, for the military to procure lots of them. One problem to address is that current versions break down frequently, particularly in inclement weather.

SUGVs will be used largely for tactical surveillance, sometimes in tandem with airborne vehicles. The Packbots deployed in Afghanistan are being outfitted with lenses to detect land mines. Biochemical sensors could detect biological or chemical agents. Upon recognizing a threat, the UGV will be able to call in strikes from unmanned and piloted aircraft. The small robots will be outfitted with a variety of frequencies, for reliable transmission under varying conditions, according to National Defense magazine. In urban warfare situations, low radio frequencies will permit sending messages inside buildings. In open terrain, higher frequencies could be switched on.

Another SUGV-type variant under development is the DARPA-funded Raptor (Robotic Autonomous Perception Technology for Off Road), a project of SAIC. Raptor is a dune buggy-like vehicle with intelligent navigation software that sports both passive and active sensors. It is a so-called "marsupial" system - marsupial as in "kangaroo." Raptor will act as a robot mothership commanding an attached group of roving robots. In one combat scenario, Raptor would be airdropped into enemy territory, where the mothership would release its family of small robots. These smaller bots would deploy like a squad of human commandos, traversing the terrain using night vision lenses and laser radar to accurately map out surroundings, according to National Defense. They would send collected intelligence to the mothership for assembly and transmission back to base.

Engineers at Draper Laboratory, a MIT spin-off in Cambridge, Massachusetts, are working on military robots even smaller than the Raptor's swarm. These "throwbots" are tossable robots the size and shape of a grapefruit that a G.I. could hurl into a building suspected of harboring hostile forces. Once inside, the diminutive robot will rove about on spiked wheels, transmitting video from its embedded camera. A soldier monitoring the video images would navigate the throwbot through radio controls.

Unmanned Ground Vehicles

The second FCS vehicle type, the Mule Unmanned Ground Vehicle (UGV), is projected to be medium-sized, weighing two tons or more. It will literally "take the Load off of' individual soldiers by transporting supplies and gear, according to John Pike of Global Security. The Army hopes it can get UGVs up and running in three years.

One Mule variant under development, the Robotic Infantry Support System, will provide water purification, battery recharging, a medical station, and top-level sensor and communications platforms. Similarly, the team of Lockheed Martin, BAE Systems, and Sandia National Labs are building a 1,500-pound vehicle that might fit the parameters of the Mule UGV.

UGV development projects are not limited to Mules alone. DARPA is funding a number teams to develop different types of Unmanned Ground Combat Vehicles (UGCVs) that are expected to be able to range up to 300 miles. The $5.5 million Spinner initiative provides one example. Spinner is a six-wheeled, five-ton unmanned prototype built by Being and PEl Electronics of Huntsville. The National Robotics Engineering Consortium (NREC) of Carnegie Mellon University is coordinating the development of the all-terrain, crash-resistant vehicle, according to project chief John Bares.

The Spinner's six independently suspended wheels, each with its own high-torque, liquid-cooled electric motor, enable it to perform its resupply or recon missions, "including the ability to operate while it's inverted," noted Bares. If its flips over, the Spinner can right itself by reorienting its wheels 180 degrees. Ireland-based Timoney Technology designed the unique traction system. PEl Electronics formulated the lithium-ion power pack supported by a diesel-fuel turbine engine.

Armed Reconnaissance Vehicles

Armed Reconnaissance Vehicles (ARV), which can act as weapons platforms, will be the most expensive of the three Future Combat System robotic land vehicle types. One five-ton ARV being developed by General Dynamics could contain 30-mm guns, as well as Hellfire missiles. The ARV might operate autonomously or be directed by a soldier-controller. A reconnaissance version of the ARV may also be produced.

More prosaic is the CyberGuard robot, manufactured by Virginia-based Cybermation. CyberGuard randomly patrols warehouses for private companies. The Pentagon wants to procure and arm CyberGuard with pepper-spray-like weapons.

Navy Efforts

Although the Army dominates the unmanned land vehicle arena, the Navy is also moving forward on underwater, shoreline, and ground robots.

Long in development, the Robart program of the Navy's SPAWAR (Space and Naval Warfare) initiative has progressed from a single, watch guard-style robot that could detect intruders, to one that can assess a situation, and finally on to a mechanized weapon that can fire back at interlopers. The latest version, the Robart III, is equipped with a pneumatic dart gun that can fire six rubber bullets or tranquilizer darts within ten seconds, according to SPAWAR.

Robart possesses a unique firing mechanism that bonds the camera and drive control to the gun to ensure the robot targets where the weapon is pointed. Few intruders will get past Robart's complex of sensors - a microwave motion detector, an infrared proximity sensor, sonar transducers, and a surveillance camera. Navy researchers are attempting to turn the single Robart machine into a proactive group of robots. In the master/slave network that is envisioned, companion bots would accompany Robart into a war-torn site to serve as lookouts and datarelay points.

Another Navy effort, the $50 million Spartan project, is an Advanced Concept Technology program designed to develop four prototypes of a surface platform geared for operation in littoral areas. The 10-foot-long, operator-controlled vehicles will move at 14 mph conducting surveillance. It will also carry a ton-and-half of payload to execute mine clearing. The Spartan's contractors - Northrup Grumman, Raytheon, and Integrated Maritime Platforms International - plan to deploy the Spartan UGV by 2007.

The Navy hopes to conduct mine sweeping operations underwater as well. Operating over the horizon from US naval vessels, the Remote Minehunting System (RMS) will detect and record mines that are moored or on the sea bottom. Anti-submarine warfare is another potential mission. The contractors for the $130 million RMS program are Lockheed Martin, Raytheon, Harris, A rete , and BAE.

Another intriguing project is Draper Laboratory's "robotic tuna", or VCUUV (Vorticity Control Unmanned Undersea Vehicle). With the appearance and maneuverability of a yellowfin tuna, the VCUUV will be able to swim underwater at depths of 100 feet for up to three hours.

Technical Challenges

Much hard research remains if robots are to fulfil the considerable demands of the military branches. According to Army Lieutenant Colonel (retired) John Blitch, who led the robot search effort at Ground Zero, and is widely considered the godfather of the military's land robot programs, future military robotic devices will have to be able to comply with his Five Imperatives:

"A Tactical Mobile Robot must be able to get back on its feet when it has fallen. It must be able to recover from communication loss. It must know where it is. It must be tamperproof. And it must be able to maneuver around complex obstacles."

National Academy of Sciences would add another imperative to the Blitch five integration, particularly data integration. The 2002 NAS report on Army unmanned vehicles concludes "the greatest technical challenge for fielding UGVs is likely to be technology integration," including the integration of the many sensors a robot could carry.

Autonomous Operation

Robots have progressed from radio-controlled devices always in sight of their human handlers to tele-assisted machines that can transmit data from a far, with occasional adjustment from their handlers. A key goal now is construction of robots that can perform whole missions independent of human intervention.

Artificial intelligence will playa critical role in autonomous operation. Research in this area is moving along on a number of fronts. For example, SAIC engineers are designing software in which a robot's arrays of sensors upload incoming data to other sensors to generate a set of directives. The processed information is then passed on to more sophisticated software that decides on a course of action for the robot.

DARPA's Information Processing Technology Office is planning research on cognitive software systems that will attempt to mimic the human mind in making sense of changing, unpredictable situations. Drawing on the work of psychologists and philosophers, such systems, the Agency hopes, will set priorities, learn from experiences, adjust to surprises, plan for the future, and make use of context to determine the optimal response. Also working in this field is the Navy Center for Applied Research in AI, which stresses the incorporation of continuous learning and constantly evolving behaviours in its robotic software.

Turning to the Natural World

Perhaps the most surprising area of research into autonomous operation involves the natural world. To improve the mobility and intelligence of its machines, the military is applying lessons culled from insects and other animals. Again, DARPA is in the fore, through its Defense Sciences Office's three-year Controlled Biological and Biomimetic Systems program. The Office of Naval Research is another sponsor.

Researchers hope to use creatures directly, or adapt their behaviours in robots. Moths might be trained to detect chemical weapons, for example. Beetles might lead to improved sensors, as the bugs can sense a fire from 40 miles away with their natural smoke detection mechanisms.

Scientists are also trying to apply to robots the manner in which animals move through challenging terrain. Lobsters, Northeastern University researchers have found, keep their balance in pounding surf by, in effect, skiing with their legs. Geckos walk across ceilings by peeling and sticking back on their feet. McGill University's Center for Intelligent Machines has concluded that, for stability at least, four or more legs are better than two. A multiple of mechanical legs might also beat treads when it comes to getting up steep hillsides. NASA's Jet Propulsion Laboratory is developing five-jointed mechanical snakes and tiny robotic worms that could slither through ruined buildings.

Just the Beginning

The emphasis on homeland security, causality reduction during combat and cost savings has pushed robots and robotic research onto the fast track for government spending. The expected result is that future military forces will employ a variety of robotic devices for reconnaissance and surveillance, logistics and support, and offensive operations. Given the Pentagon's vast, well-funded and long-term robot program, many more discoveries, applications, and business opportunities will result from the application of robotics in the service of military operations.

Ed Moser, based in Alexandria, Virginia, is a *writer and editor of articles, speeches, newsletters, and books on science, information science, national security, business, and politics. He can be reached at mosered@iuno. com.*

US Fighting Strength to be 1/3 Robotic By 2015

For generations of science fiction writers the idea of robotic hordes ruling the battlefield has been fertile ground for their active imaginations. From "Star Wars" to "The Terminator", the rise of these machines has been the fodder for some great entertainment.

But while these extraordinary machines have captured our imagination in both film and print, the reality of battlefield robots is being played out on battlefields all over the globe.

More R2D2 than C3PO, today's military robots are playing life saving roles in both Afghanistan and Iraq. They fulfill missions either too dangerous or impossible for humans to perform themselves. In the process they not only give U.S. troops the tactical advantage but also save precious lives.

In fact, the contributions of military robots have become so important to the forces in the field that the machines are quickly becoming as commonplace and accepted as the rifle itself.

And it is a tactical trend whose weight in value continues to soar. So much so that by 2015 the U.S. Department of Defense has projected that a full 1/3 of its future fighting force will be made up entirely of robots.

It's all part of $127 billion project, known as Future Combat Systems that is being developed by the Defense Advanced Research Agency (DARPA), whose mission is to ensure that the U.S forces maintain their technological superiority. It is a transformation that is one of the largest technology missions ever undertaken in American history.

* * * Rumsfeld's Going Away Gift. . . a $214 Million Order for America's New Ultimate Combat Vehicle

This new armored vehicle eats IEDs for lunch. In fact, not a single American soldier in Iraq has ever been killed while inside these vehicles.

The Pentagon is buying so many, the company's stock is up 1,011 % for the year. But the gains are just getting started.

Here's my personal 100% satisfaction guarantee to you. If this stock doesn't gain at least 500% in the next 12 months, you can ask for a complete refund on your subscription.

But while the exploits of the many unmanned aerial drones are now part of the common understanding, it is the ground variants of these machines that are paying dividends to the boots on the ground today.

Led by robots such as the TALON, produced by Foster Miller, and various smaller robots made by iRobot (IRBT:NASDAQ), these new machines are hard at work protecting the troops from their enemies.

The TALON, in fact, played a large role in the now famous battle of Tora Bora. These heavily armed mini-tanks were sent into the areas where humans feared to tread, dispatching AI-Qaida fighters and searching for the Bin Laden himself.

And while these machines never did find our elusive arch enemy, they did prove themselves to be an effective alternative to putting troops at risk.

Today these same types of machines are also being put to use in Iraq. Along with the TALON, smaller variants of these robots have proven themselves time and time again.

Among them are the man-portable iRobot Packbot Tactical EOD Mobile Robot designed to eliminate the dangerous improvised explosive devices that have been so harmful to our troops in Iraq.

Developed by the same company that produces the famous Roomba robotic vacuum cleaner, about 300 of these Packbots have been deployed in Iraq. Since then they have been involved thousands of Explosive Ordinance Device (EOD) missions.

These rugged track wheeled devices are controlled by users on the ground using the same type of joystick controls that are commonplace among video games. Working form the safety of a vehicle soldiers use a monitor to guide the robot to the weapon and are able to disable it without having to go to the extreme of sending in a man with a clunky bomb suit.

The bottom line for these robotic exploits is saved American lives. As a Navy chief said commenting on a Packbot destroyed in the line of duty, "When a robot dies you don't have to write a letter to its mother."

Other robots produced by the company include the PackBot Scout and the Packbot Explorer, which allow soldiers to perlonn reconnaissance and surveillance missions from safe positions.

The company has even teamed up with John Deere to produce a ground vehicle based on the popular M-Gator design. The autonomous vehicle is designed to serve numerous important roles including acting as an unmanned scout, a perimeter guard, and a supply carrier. Versions of the prototype are currently being produced and could see battlefield action in the near future.

But not all of these new robots are designed to search and destroy. Some even work to save lives directly. In fact, one new device is designed to bring wounded soldiers off of the battlefield and has been funded by Congress to the tune of $1.1 million for 2007.

Built by Vecna Robotics, the Battlefield Extraction-Assist Robot (BEAR) has hydraulic anus that can support injured soldiers weighing up to 400 lbs. Its system of wheels and tracks allow it to climb up hills or roll over rough terrain while staying low to the ground. Working from a safe position its controllers will be able to rescue the wounded without exposing the unit's medics to hostile fire.

But as amazing and as important as these current robots are, they are nothing compared to the machines that DARPA is working on and will deploy in the future. The truth is that by 2035 the U.S. Military plans to march its first force made up entirely of autonomous robot/soldiers onto the battlefield. And when they do, the Terminator of movie fame will be that much closer to reality.

It's the beginning of a brave new world one in which soldiers no longer have the monopoly on death and dying.

Let's just hope that all of those science fiction writers aren't as prophetic as they are entertaining because the rise of the machines is an unstoppable trend in military thinking.

A NATO workshop on short-term realizable military robots

In military robotics, industry has a rather leading role in defining the military use of robotics. Often more or less standard robots are introduced into the military operations without very thoroughly defined military functional requirements. These standard robots are then tested on how they function in a military operational environment. To the opinion of the NATO working group IST-032/RTG-0141, this is an undesired situation that needs improvement.

Therefore, the working group organized a workshop in Bonn, Germany to bring together military users, industry and researchers and bridge the gap on robotics between military users, industry and researchers. A final outcome of the workshop would be a roadmap, indicating what gaps between military user requirements for robotics and industrial robotic capabilities are to be expected in the year 2008, what actions should be taken to close those gaps in time, and who should take action. It was recognized during the workshop that this was the first time such an integral analysis was made.

The workshop consisted of several meetings during three days and was attended by about 70 people from the military, industry, research and government, from sixteen mainly European countries.

Military tasks and requirements

Starting point in the workshop was defining the tasks for which the military would most like to have robotic support by the year 2008, including the functional requirements. This would put user requirements upfront the process of bridging the gap between military users, industry and research.

The five most relevant tasks identified were are explained here.

Task 1: Reconnaissance and surveillance for tactical support for the forces on the ground including NBC

In this task, the users envisage to use a single UGV (Unmanned Ground Vehicle) for zone, area, route and point reconnaissance. By combining these various activities in a single UGV, users try to explicitly indicate that they would prefer a UGV that can be used in multiple settings.

Users want the UGV tot give them information about location and movement of persons and vehicles (civil and military), including as much as possible an Identification Friend or Foe (IFF) indication. The UGV should also provide information on NBC contaminated locations and map information on routes. It should warn the operator when a threat for an area of responsibility is detected.

Users also made requirements about potential use under all weather conditions, in all climates and in all sorts of terrain. This sort of UGV is likely to merge information from various sensors and vehicles and should give the operator only information when relevant. The UGV should be able to communicate with other manned or unmanned vehicles to point targets and to identify persons and vehicles with high reliability, and it should have sufficient capabilities to protect itself.

Task 2: De-mining - Tactical and post-conflict - clearing l'oads and fields from AP and AT mines

In the de-mining UGV, users envisage to combine different types of de-mining that are currently distinct disciplines. Especially tactical and post-conflict de-mining have quite different requirements in de-mining speed and de-mining accuracy.

[1]IST-032/RTG-014 is called "Multi-robot systems in military domains" Although this group's primary focus is on multi-robot systems, in the September 2004 workshop focus

was put on single robots instead. This is caused by the quite short time horizon of the workshop, looking into robot, being available in the year 2008, while multi-robots are not expected to be close to being functional by then.

This UGV should be capable of detecting all types of anti-personnel (AP) and anti-tank (AT) mines and optionally mark the mines. Wherever possible, the UGV should either remove the mine or disarm it in place. When a mine is found, the UGV should warm the operator and also provide the mine's location and type, including the estimated time and success rate to clear the mine. Optionally, the UGV should inform the operator when the mine is marked or disanned. It should be possible to operate the UGV both in a teleoperated and in an autonomous mode when clearing the assigned area or route. The UGV should be usable on all kinds of roads and fields as well as in urban terrain. It should operate under all climatic and weather conditions. The UGV should be able to receive and use airbome information on possible mine locations.

Task 3: Convoying - transport of goods

In this task, the military envisage to use UGVs in a convoy for transport of goods both on roads and in heavy terrain to reach non-compound troops. This type of UGV should be able to transport goods in an adequate time, meaning in a time comparable to that of a human driver.

The UGV should either be capable of loading and unloading itself or be capable to be handled by one or more specialized UGVs in the convoy. The location of the convoy should be known at all times. The UGV must be able to follow a non-physically linked, man driven vehicle and it must also be able to move autonomously, whereby the operator should be able to take over control at any time. To the users, an acceptable solution would be a leader-follower vehicle concept.

Highly important is the capability of this type of UGV to mix in normal traffic, including all legal issues involved.

Task 4: Checking vehicles and people for explosives and weapons at checkpoints

This type of UGV should approach a suspected vehicle or person and search for weapons and explosives.

When found, the UGV should alert the operator and keep the vehicle and person from moving away. The UGV should be able to shield off an explosion for own forces or buildings. It should also be able to identify the type of explosive and alert all persons in the vicinity of the explosive. The typical working environment for this UGV is at checkpoints, meaning that it is to be operated on a road. For optimal usability, the UGV should memorize cars and persons spotted at the checkpoint for analysis later on.

Task 5: Carry equipment for dismounted soldier

This UGV is meant to carry the equipment and supplies of a small number of soldiers. Users indicated that it should also be usable to transport wounded soldiers.

The UVG should be able to follow soldiers nearly anywhere they go and therefore it should be usable in all terrains. It should be possible to operate the UGV from a distance, for instance to make the purposely left behind UGV drive up to the soldiers as soon as the operational situation is safe enough. To be useful, the UGV must operate for at least 48 hours on a stretch, and preferably should weigh less than 100 kilograms. Users indicated that the UGV should be able to provide power to the squad equipment and should also be a communication up-link. The UGV should have self defence against thieves, and should memorize who touched it.

Technological gaps and the way to close them

During the workshop, industry and researchers defined

the current status of technology and the level of technology that is expected to be achieved by the year 2008 at the current speed of technological development. For this purpose, six technological groups were organised along the lines of six different fields of technological interest.

Together with military users, these technological groups also identified the gaps they foresee for the year 2008 between user requirements and the then expected technology status. After that, roadmaps were constructed that identify which actions should be taken in order to achieve the required level of technology by 2008. It was also identified who should take action and how this should be organized.

The outcome of this process is described below for each of these: six technological groups.

Communication

Communication is essential for the use of all kinds of robot systems. In most cases, especially when using multi-robot systems where several robots deliberately co-operate in an autonomous manner, there is a demand for wireless communication to achieve high flexibility. In single robot systems, the communication system is usually used to control the robot and to get information from the system sensors (e.g. vision, radar, et cetera). For example, in a reconnaissance and surveillance scenario the task is to gather information about the surrounding area of the robot system. Multi-robot systems combine the functionality of single robot systems to achieve a higher efficiency and to cope with scenarios that are more complex; in the surveillance scenario example an object could be observed by a multi-robot system from different positions and with different sensors. Through the results of a sensor data fusion process, it would be possible to get a more complete and exhaustive situation awareness than achievable with only one robot or sensor. Because of cooperating robot systems, there is a high diversity of demands for the communication system.

The following demands on the communication system were identified:

- mobile and wireless ad-hoc communication;
- high ranges;
- high data rates;
- multipoint communication;
- adjustment to the varying availability of the network;
- compliance with Quality of Service (QoS) demands;
- prioritization of data;
- secure communication;
- power awareness.

A generic robot communication system should meet these requirements but today's technology does not support all of these requirements at the same time. Satellite communication for example may allow high data rates over a long distance but there is no solution for a moving robot system. Additionally, most satellite antennas are too big for up to medium robot systems. Other technologies like HF, UHF, and VHF do support high ranges but lack high data rates. GSM, GPRS and UMTS do support medium and high data rates but are in need of an existing infrastructure that either may be under foreign control or does not even exist in the area of operation. Communication technologies like Wireless LAN, Laser or Infrared support ad-hoc communication and high data rates, but have their own weaknesses.

Overall, the currently available communication technologies cannot support all of the above requirements and it is unlikely that a single communication technology may support all of the requirements in 2008. Thus, a new communication approach for robot systems may have to combine different communication technologies. Possibly the integration of the Software Defined Radio (SDR) concept will be of advantage. Another promising approach would be the development of special mobile ad-hoc network (MANET) protocols that focus on covering all the requirements mentioned above. As such, a protocol usually works as a routing protocol on the IP layer it could benefit from improvements on lower layers, for example the integration of the SDR concepts.

Robot Platforms

The robotic platform is the glue that holds together all the other aspects of a fieldable tactical military unmanned ground vehicle. Unless the platform exhibits a high degree of mobility and outstanding ruggedness it will fail to achieve its target location. If the UGV can not deploy its sensors at the correct location then the mission is rendered useless.

The platform should merge the drive system, a power supply system sufficient for the required mission period, an advanced communication system capable of returning real-time information to the user and a user friendly Human Machine Interface (HMI) that allows long term, stress free operations. The platform must have a very high immunity to electro-magnetic interference, and logistically any tactical UGV must not impose a heavy load on available systems or manpower.

As all these functions rely on the chassis or platform to hold the system together, any new tactical platform must be modular in concept. Like the aircraft and scientific industries who already have standards on shape and hole mounting patterns we should strive to arrive at a common standard such that any type of sensor pack could be incorporated into a UGV of a given size. Mounting the sensor is but a part of the integration problem; all equipment requires power, which must be supplied via a connector. Standardizations on power supplies and connectors joining platforms and equipment together would be an advantage.

For near term tactical robotic platforms following developments are needed:

1) develop and integrate the latest power cell technology into the UGV;

2) adopt the latest very high efficiency motor drives and power train systems to give very high mobility even when damaged;

3) refine wheeled and track transmission and suspensions systems (the author thinks that in the near term fieldable walking remote control vehicles will not be possible, however these are a long term aspiration);

4) use of new materials and building methods to reduce mass yet retain performance, including ballistic protection;

5) development of HMI system to ensure tactical robots do not give a high work load on user;

6) develop an EMC hardening program to ensure C3 systems operate in real world battle space.

In short develop modular platforms that can continue to support the array of sensors and other equipment necessary to prosecute a mission. Be able to adapt to new technologies, be fully integrated into the tactical 1STAR scheme and operate in the real world.

While the near tenn looks at developing and extending current systems the long term should be looking into achieving what has been identified as a tactical need today but can not yet be realised:

1) The users identified that an ideal tactical UGV platform should be capable of going wherever a man can go. Currently no fieldable UGV can jump across a deep ditch or leap through a window. While laboratory grade walking humanoid robots exist they are far from fieldable in a tactical environment.

2) Development of highly dextrous humanoid robotics similar to those proposed for the International Space Station would allow any vehicle or plant currently driven by a human to be operated under remote control without the need to modify the vehicle. While laboratory experiments and small scale field trials are currently taking place these will need time and funding to mature into fieldable robotics.

3) Research facilities have demonstrated autonomous and semi-autonomous operations ofUGVs under laboratory conditions as well as swarming and co-operative operations between groups of UGVs or UA Vs. These concepts show promise for future operations but is not thought mature enough yet to be fieldable in a real world scenario, for these to mature they too will need funding.

Sensing and Wodd Modelling

The mission success of any robot highly depends on its sensors and world model. The quality of sensor gathered information is important for tele-operated robots that pass this information directly to an operator, but also and even more for autonomous robots that use their sensor information for autonomous navigation and all sorts of autonomous mission dependent information collection subtasks. A good world model is a 'must have' for autonomous robots as this is the robot's total view on the 'outside world' and thus the robot's basis for coherent navigation and execution of mission tasks.

Good sensors and world model are essential for basic information on the robot's own location and movements, but also for tasks like region observation, route planning or automated detection and recognition of typical targets. The right sensors to use depend on the actual tasks to perform. Examples of current sensors are infrared (imaging) sensors, (I-ID)TV/CCD-sensors, laser and acoustic sensors and even radar antennas or arrays including mini-SAR (depending on the size of the robot).

Because of the variety of conditions that robots will be operated in, most sensors should be usable under all weather and environmental conditions and in all sorts of terrain. For many tasks the information should be processed on-board of the UGA, and should be effective and efficient by means of information compression and filtering of relevant information.

Concerning sensors and world modelling for military robots, following gaps were identified:

1) Obstacle avoidance and negotiation, terrain modelling and classification, and transport in normal traffic, including unstructured terrain. This gap is considered vital as it deternlines the vehicle's basic capabilities for navigation, and can only be partly solved by 2008.

2) Mine detection, de-mining, chemical and biological sensing (nuclear detection and identification at contact range is considered solved). This gap is considered not vital but important.

3) Environmental mapping, sensor fusion at limited visibility, situational awareness as well as human and vehicle detection and recognition. This gap is considered to be solved in research forums for civil applications, and knowledge to be transferred to military applications. In that sense, this gap is not of relevance for a military robot road map.

The greatest challenge will be in multi-sensor suites including sensor fusion, meaning that information from diverse sensors (for instance video and radar) on the UGV is analyzed and then merged into a more complete and robust view on the robot's 'outside world' than can be achieved by any single sensor. Also technological solutions for all weather and environmental conditions and variations of (complex structured) terrain are a challenge. Sensor fusion within reconnaissance vehicles including navigation and mission planning is seen as matured in 2008.

Navigation and Mission Planning

This section includes three different aspects that should be differentiated. Starting from the top level we have the Mission Planning, the Path planning and the Navigation. Mission Planning is mission specific and considerably changes according to the scenario.

Starting with the data provided by the Mission Planning, the Path Planning produces paths and waypoints taking into account the kinematics and dynamic capabilities of the robots involved in the mission. The Navigation consists in avoiding those obstacles while following the initial paths. In order to avoid or pass obstacles and to recover from small path changes (obstacles avoidance and passing) the robots must be equipped with distance and position sensors. Control architectures for Navigation are generally deliberative, meaning that there is a strong coupling between the sensors data and the motion commands sent to the robot actuators. These architectures are based on simple behaviours that are combined using Behaviour Coordination Mechanisms (BCM). In order to implement co-ordination, the system must at least provide the following capabilities: sensor information distribution and distributed behaviour communication and coordination mechanisms (for example through standard Message Passing Protocols like JAUS).

When analyzing the five selected military tasks, several navigation aspects were found vital for military purposes but not yet foreseen to be solved by the year 2008 under the current development speed. Therefore following vital gaps were found in the field of navigation and mission planning:

- autonomous road following;
- autonomous driving in mixed traffic (max speed of 50 km/h);
- moving in all terrains with tactical behaviour in (nearly) all weather conditions;
- following leader (manned or autonomous), any type of vehicle.

To achieve the roadmap, following has to be done in the coming years:

- concept and agree on real target scenarios, prioritise different driving conditions; .
- decide on and develop experimental systems;
- organise trials (from lab to field prototype to fully operational);
- define performance measures;
- improve navigation technology through experimental systems;
- manage a navigation technology group;
- develop coordination and interaction with other technology groups;
- find funds.

Human-robot Interaction

While mastering the operation of a fully manually controlled UGV usually is a simple task and operators can be trained effectively using existing equipment, for a realistic combat environment fully manual control was found to be insufficient. This is caused by the emerging operator fatigue and lack of awareness of combat activities at his site. In order to keep the soldier operator aware of the battle development and to allow him to react quickly to improve his personal safety, it is mandatory to shorten the current very long delay needed for the human operator to adapt himself from the remotely monitored environment back to the local real world. Fully manual control does work fine for training of non-experts and for maintaining the capabilities of already well trained operators.

For adequate remote operation in a military operation environment, it is mandatory to upgrade from a continuous manually remote controlled system into a supervised autonomous one. This approach is used by so-called telerobots.

For training systems using Agent Based Systems, the current technology level is at a relatively preliminary state for enabling training of non-experts. In very short periods of time, as well as the feasibility to develop such equipment in less than three years. The opinion in the workshop was that the technology is well understood and similar systems are operational in other relevant areas. We assumed that training non-experts for operating relatively sophisticated equipment, like the telerobots, would take one month and that operation is feasible to be done in the next years.

The group considered different aspects of human-robot-interaction including:

- workload/occupation level for operator performing basic UGV control in simple/ difficult terrain;
- substituting/supporting UGV operator training/ instructing using interactive simulations;

- evaluating the performance of the human-robot team;
- defining measures of effectiveness for the human-robot team;
- consistent interface design for different UGVs for common UGV functions (on/off, manoeuvring, parking etc.), consisting of:
- standardized controls (e.g. manoeuvring);
- standardized symbolic representation (e.g. ISO, DIN, MIL based symbols);
- standardized layout or sub-layouts for interface components.
- providing robot execution plan to operator ahead of manoeuvre;
- scaling operator to robot ratio on demand (adapting to unexpected workload peaks);
- no limitations on interaction caused by UGV loosing line of sight (LOS) contact with operator is seen by the users as an important feature;
- no degradation of performance (e.g. speed, accuracy) for basic UGV control when operator is wearing protective gloves/ vest/ full ABC protection.

Following technical issues were found vital to solve before 2008:

- workload/occupation level less than 50% for operator performing basic UGV control in simple terrain / difficult terrain (75%);
- providing robot execution plan to operator ahead of manoeuvre:
- development of appropriate wearable user interface;

- evaluating the performance and measures of effectiveness of the human-robot team.

Some other issues were considered not vital, but nevertheless important to be solved:

- important issue: scaling operator to robot ratio on demand (adapting to unexpected workload peaks)
- important issue: consistent interface design for different UGVs for common UGV functions (standardized symbolic representation, standardized layout.). Also scaling operator to robot ratio on demand (adapting to unexpected workload peaks);
- important issue: Non-degradation of performance because of use of any protective equipment (gloves, vest, NBC gear).

Multi-robot Systems

A multi-robot system is a system, comprising more than one robot, in which the tasks and activities of the multi-robot system are shared between the robots. The nature of the task sharing could range from simple workload sharing, or distributed sensing, to more complex co-operative or collaborative behaviours. The architecture of the multi-robot system could be fully distributed or it could have a hierarchical command and control structure.

Several multi-robot systems research projects have been performed, such as projects funded by the US, DARPA, which are all aimed at fulfilling reconnaissance or surveillance scenarios. A famous example is Cognitive Colonies, a project that uses robots for reconnaissance tasks (see picture). In Europe, many projects, e.g. Martha and Corom, tried to develop obstacle avoidance and anti-collision between units or co-ordination and adaptivity. All projects are still at an exploratory stage, meaning that there are no current operational examples of multi-robot systems in the strategic domain. Therefore, it is important to note that multi-robot systems relate to a potential rather than an actual technology.

Using several initial assumptions - particularly concerning the level of autonomy - and focusing on scenarios relevant for multi-robot systems "Reconnaissance and surveillance for tactical support", "Demining - tactical and post-conflict" and "Convoying, transport of goods", the following vital technology gaps were identified in relation to multi-robot systems:

i To interact with other robots performing different, specialized tasks.

ii To perform a task with multiple, collaborative robots.

iii To autonomously divide a task, specified by the operator, between several robots.

iv Cooperative Perception: to collectively recognise objects of interest.

v The ability to autonomously manage and prioritise events.

vi Co-operative Perception: the ability to share data from multiple sources.

vii To interact with other robots performing exactly the same task.

Work on most of these issues should start immediately and a new research program- in which the research and industry communities work together - should be established on multi-robot interaction. In fact, they already do work together, but a lack of funding prevents desirable progress. A problem is that military users are interested in multi-robot systems but still have to consolidate funding. Another problem is that current multi-robot system research is ad hoc, as there is no real 'user pull'.

A solution to this might be a European version of the US DARPA, being a private/public co-operation. This organisation should lobby for funding and define research demands. The initiative for such a priyate/public co-operation should come from military users in the various countries, in mutual cooperation. This could be part of WEAG or OCCAR.

Follow-up: The Core Group

In order to keep the integrating outcomes of the workshop alive, it was decided at the workshop to establish a so-called Core Group, consisting of users, industry and researchers. Although the users initially consist of only military, other users that have related tasks are also invited to participate.

The Core Group is partially a NATO activity and partially a EURON activity. with the NATO part focussing on supporting military-like tasks by robots while the EURON activity focuses on stimulating research to achieve goals relevant to the users and therefore the industry.

One of the main activities of this Core Group is the organization of a capability show, to be held in the second quarter of 2006, aiming at a closer mutual understanding on the needs and possibilities of robotics between military and industry. This capability show is to be followed by a research contest to be held in 2007 that aims to support closing the gap between research and industry. More information on the Core Group and its current activities can be found on the website www.european-robotics.org.

Authors

This publication is a joint effort of following participants.

Group	Name	Role	E-mail
Communication	F.E. Schneider	Section coordinator	Frank. Schneider@fgan. de
Human-robot interaction	R. Granot	Section coordinator	rgranot@inter. net. il

Group	Name	Role	E-mail
Human-robot interaction	J. Roning	Co-author	Juha.Roning@oulu.fi
Multi-robot systems	A. Winfield	Section coordinator	Alan. Winfield@uwe.ac. uk
Multi-robot systems	E.J.A. van Zijderveld	Co-author	Erik.vanZijderveldr@tno.nl
Multi-robot systems	L. Walle	Co-author	laurent. walle@cybemetix.fr
Navigation and mission planning	E. Colon	Section coordinator	Eric.Colon@rma.ac.be
Robot platforms	K Pink	Section coordinator	kpink I@QinetiQ.com
Robot platforms	R. Castelli	Co-author	cas telli@macroswiss.com
Sensing and world modelling	D. Krogmann	Section coordinator	Dirk. Krogmann@diehl-bgt-defence.de

5

HOW TO HANDLE TRAUMA OF ARMED ROBOT ENCOUNTER

Introduction

Men have fought wars and battles from thousand of years and for various reasons. These include the desire of power, money, land, or resources. From the same time men have utilized technology to achieve these goals at lower cost, time and effort. This has lead to a history of technological developments especially designed for army use and the involvement of some of the finest minds in military affairs. Many of these technologies like automatic guns, which were considered frontier line tools a few decades back, are now in the hands of civilians.

If the history is going to repeat itself like it has always, current war machines will also become household tools in a few decades and will be legally held by civilians. This includes, besides many other things, the robotic warriors currently being developed at various labs around the world. This perceived threat has motivated this study where we explore some issues related to robot - human encounters.

We start with a discussion of the problems associated with armed robot - human encounters in the battle field and discuss similar problems in the context of terrorist attacks. We survey the role of psychological test in military training and propose a new test. Section V gives our conclusions and recommendations.

Armed Robot - Human Encounters in the Battlefield

Although many of the problems associated with robot - human encounters are present irrespective of the environment, we like to differentiate between the two very different environments of peace and war. Encounters in each will have its own typical features which need to be explored in detail. In this section we concentrate on the scenario where a soldier faces a robot in the hostile environment of war.

We are not aware of any publicly available study conducted to understand the response of uninitiated human beings to robotic weapons. However, studies have been conducted to understand the behavior of human conducts towards a robot or a simulated figure on a computer. One such study conducted at Stanford University, [1] was focused on testing how real people respond to virtual ones, especially to their voices. The study showed that subjects were hesitant to give personal information to synthetic faces and voices compared to text based responses. The behavior is not just limited to robots or simulated figures on screen. Normal human beings, in general, find it difficult to cope with a technology that is new for them and that may require restraining or adjustments in their working styles and behaviors. It has been found that men and women resist a change to new technology, even in industrial and business environments. Extensive studies in the use of information technologies in organizations have shown this repeatedly, [2]. However the situation in the battlefield is very different. First of all, the environment is not that of peace and there are a lot of anxieties associated with war in general.

Furthermore, the untrained army soldier may not have a choice in dealing with artificial intelligence. It is also well know that even without high technology a soldier suffers from a lot of fears, indignities, and tensions. These are in addition to the problems of thirst, hunger, etc., in an environment of extreme heat or cold, months or even years of uncertainty. These problems eat away a combatant's nerves. On top of all these, the soldier is now going to handle robots.

The current generation of military robots does not 'appear' to be intelligent machines; not at least to an uneducated and uninitiated soldier. Because of this he may not feel threatened by their existence any more than a normal military vehicle. Due to the absence of human beings on top, these may be mistaken as remotely controlled vehicles. Hence we may have difficulty conducting 'real' tests on Human - Robot encounters in the battlefield.

Since real data is not available to us, let's create a hypothetical scene where a military man encounters an intelligent entity and try to think what can happen. We list the steps through which he will possibly go through:

1. An un-initiated soldier finds himself amongst war machines of various sizes and shapes.
2. He then feels that some of these machines are more than 'machines' - they are intelligent.
3. His first reaction to this would be a feeling of anxiety or panic[a].

---

[a]We use the standard definitions in psychologically: anxiety is a normal innate emotional alarm response to the *anticipation* of danger or threa. Panic is similar to anxiety but is a normal, innate emotional alarm response to the perception of *immediate* danger or threat, [3-5]. Anxiety is a natural mechanism which allows human beings to be alert in the face of unexpected events and accidents. In fact, a moderate level of anxiety can be extremely useful. I can help us to stay focused and try to solve a specific problem. But in many of the war situations the levels of anxiety are so high that the person practically freezes and hence his natural survival instincts are compromised. A diagnostic of the anxiety disorder can be made by the "Diagnostic and Statistical Manual of Mental Disorders", [9]. It shows that there are five different types of anxiety disorders:

4. As a trained soldier he knows how to control his emotions but now he has to do more and control the psychological effects of threat from a different and unknown type of intelligence. He might be an expert in reading human minds but will surely be at a disadvantage in dealing with artificial intelligence.

5. The soldier may also feel insulted (i.e., his ego may be hurt) by the fact that a sub-human entity is trying to kill him, or has already killed some of his companions. He also needs methods of assurance that this feeling of insult is temporary and can be controlled. If not, the impact of this traumatic state can be damaging for both the combatant and the nation he is serving.

6. Assuming he can control a little bit his level of anxiety or panic, his next step would be to identify intelligent entities among other, non-intelligent, machines and weapons. We give such machines the generic name of 'robot'.

---

1. Generalized Anxiety Disorder: continuous tension even in peaceful times. Minimum lasting of 6 months.
2. Panic Disorder: The patient experiments recurrent unexpected crisis of anxiety. The person usually feels his is going to die. This sudden fear attacks has no fundament reason.
3. Phobic Disorder: It is characterized by an irrational and constant fear of a specific object, activity or situation. Examples: fear of air travel, fear from birds, spiders, etc.
4. Compulsive-Obsessive Disorder: Deals with thoughts or actions that the patient does without conscious control. In such cases the person knows the absurdity of his behavior.
5. Post Traumatic Stress Disorder (PSTD): This disorder is presented in persons who were exposed to a critical traumatic experience, like a war. Patients with PTSD have constant flashbacks of the traumatic event, an emotional state of high awareness, and the general lack of interest in daily activities. The post traumatic stress disorder is experimented by 1% of the total community [10]. An increment in the digestive disorder is detected in war prisoners during the Second World War or in Korea. This could be attributed to the bad nutrition and to the infectious diseases. These symptoms are also found in war veterans, as well as in hostages with post traumatic stress disorder [11].

The Post Traumatic Stress Disorder (PTSD) was considered a clinical disorder around the 80's. It was the result of analysis of the data collected for all the symptoms presented by survivors of wars [12]. Statistics indicated that after Vietnam War, 15% of survivors had some form of PTSD while 11% showed partial symptoms.

7. Once a robot is identified or suspected (as no device is available to a soldier to do this, he has to rely on behavior patterns of the robot/machine and his instincts), he will have to think of the next step. He will have many choices: a) return to base to get help, b) see if he can destroy the robot on the spot, or c) take the most difficult decision to wait and try to understand what toe robot is doing.

If the robot is really aggressive, it would try to kill the soldier and the story ends here.

But if the robot is programmed to go closer to the enemy base and send more information to its headquarters, or to destroy a larger area rather than just a soldier, one can do more. No matter what happens afterwards, it is clear a soldier could experience emotional states that are different from the ones he is trained to deal with. That is why it might be important to design a new psychological test made to identify the profile of the soldiers and detect their flaws and weaknesses. This would help in implementing special training methods to prepare human warriors for future combats. A comprehensive program for the training and retraining of soldiers is needed to handle the emotional problems robot-human encounters may generate. We'll return to this point in a later section.

Armed Robot - Human Encounters in Terrorist Attacks

Terrorism is an old phenomena dating back, at least, to the days of Roman Empire. In the first century B.C. the Jewish terrorists used daggers against their victims as a first step to inciting a revolt against the Roman Empire, [17]. At that time daggers were considered to be a technological innovation. Other early terrorist include Hindu Thugs and the Muslim Assassins, [18] who utilized the available technologies of their times to achieve their goals. The nature and character of terrorism has changed over centuries and continue to do so. The world wide indicators show that terrorism is on the rise. Although the number of such attacks has decreased, the number of casualties has increased more than 20 times. This is due to some high-profile lethal incidents that killed more humans in one go than many incidents of the previous decades, [18]. Targets of these attacks include all nations, religions and groups. Some experts also suggest that US nationals consistently have been the most targeted since 1968, [19]. With the growing interest of terrorist organizations in the use of technology to make their attack more lethal and difficult to trace, the prospects of a technology backfire have grown further.

There is one factor that may limit the use of robotic technologies in near future. One of the four trends in modern terrorism include: an apparent increase in the incidence of religiously motivated attacks, a decrease in the overall number of attacks, an increase in the lethality per attack, and the growing targeting of Americans, [18]. Knowing the current sate of art in the field of robotics, one can see that the lethality of attacks cannot easily be increased by simply incorporating robots. For example, if the information publicly available about the developments in military robots is correct and up-to-date, the current generation of robots is not capable of reproducing incidents at the scale of World Trade Center event of September 11. A more plausible use for them would be in underdeveloped nations, where the mere news of a robot roaming around may create a lot of unrest among the population and a feeling of hatred for those developing and using these technologies. It is also possible, though doesn't seem to be very probable, to put lethal weapons / arms directly on mobile robots and let them take the decision of firing / triggering them at the right time. This may include the use of Anthrax type chemicals which can be taken close to enemy lines by an autonomous and released when triggered. The recent attacks by AI-Qaeda all show a clear desire and an expertise in the use of technology to disrupt global peace. As pointed. Out by Cronin, an examination of evidence taken from Afghanistan and Pakistan reveals AI Qaeda's interest in chemical, biological, and nuclear weapons, [18]. Admittedly this robot is far from the fanciful and sometimes ruthless robots shown in science fiction movies and hence is not expected to catch the imagination of terrorists.

The main problem in dealing with a robot-terrorist, let's say inside a building, would be the defiance of all established police rules and techniques to distract the attention of a human terrorist. The robot-terrorist will also refuse to take any advice or threat and may go to the point of attack very quickly. It is therefore important to train the army and police forces to handle autonomous robots in case of terrorist attacks. This is not an easy task since such technologies are not easily available for training purposes. Simulated games can be an effective tool in teaching armies of the third world in dealing with such situations. The developments in virtual reality have opened new frontiers and now it is possible to develop war games with Artificial Intelligence and robots in it. Such simulated worlds will provide ample opportunities to train soldiers. Such training will prove immensely valuable in case of war with another country using these technologies but also in the case of terrorist attacks.

Military Applications of Psychological Tests

For centuries humans have been tested in one way or the other for their suitability for combat jobs. Even in the 5th century B.C. the Chinese knew the importance of Psychology in warfare. Although we are not aware of any tests made for this purpose, Sun Tzu, the famous Chinese general and the author of the famous book on the subject of warfare, [6] did point out the uses of psychology. In USA for over 75 years the armed forces have pursued a policy of assessing the mental ability of adults who are eligible for military service, [7]. The first such systems was used during World War I when some 1.9 million men were tested on the Army Alpha test of intelligence for literates, and the Army Beta test of intelligence for illiterates and non-English speakers. The alpha test was designed to sample a soldier's abilities in the following areas (each comprising a subtest):

1. Following Oral Directions,
2. Arithmetical Problems,
3. Practical Judgment,
4. Synonyms-Antonyms,
5. Disarranged Sentences,
6. Number Series Completion,
7. Analogies,
8. Information.

To get a final score, results from each are combined into one grade (A, B, C+, C, C-, D or D-), with A representing a superior intelligence and D- an inferior intelligence. As can be seen, the test was rudimentary in its nature and was clearly lacking subject areas related to the use of technologies. But this helped, at least during World War I, to recruit soldiers and assign them to suitable tasks. Those who were illiterate (or with only a few years of school education) or were not good in English were asked to give the Army Beta Test. For obvious reasons, the test was designed to be completed without reading or writing by just marking answers in paper using pencils. It was composed of:

1. Maze,
2. Cube Analysis,
3. X-Q Series,

4. Digit Symbol,

5. Number Checking,

6. Picture Completion,

7. Geometrica I Construction.

With the passage of time, changing global political and war scenarios and increasing levels of education and technology, the mental ability tests have been changed in content and in the definition of what they measure. But the essence of the work has not changed - they still represent attempts to assess the cognitive skills of adults. This information is used to select people for military service and to assign them to work for which their 'aptitudes' suit them.

In World War II, the Army General Classification Test (AGCT) was used for classifying recruits to assign them different jobs. This was developed with the understanding that intelligence mayor may not measure native mental capacity. These tests can measure abilities only if everyone giving the test had equal opportunity and equal incentive to develop the abilities measured, [13]. So the army developed tests to measure the general learning ability of recruits in the following areas:

1. Vocabulary,

2. Arith metic,

3. Block-Counting.

Once again the subsets were combined and give grades from I to V, [13]. The Armed Forces Qualification Test (AFQT) was specially designed and developed to serve as a test for screening out low mental ability persons for all military services. With some changes in content, the AFQT test has remained as the primary screening test for military service through the Korean and Vietnam Wars, and up to the present, [6-8].

In developing this test care was taken to make certain that speed was not emphasized, so that there was no penalization to slow workers. Another important feature was the verbal instructions which were not so hard to follow. In 1950, the AFQT subtests were:

1. Vocabulary test,
2. Mathematics test,
3. Block-Counting test,
4. Spatial test.

From 1953 to 1973, the AFQT retained three of the subtests, Vocabulary, Mathematics, and Spatial, but the Block-Counting test was dropped in favor of a new Mechanical ability test called the 'Tool Recognition test', [14]. This was a clear step in the direction of testing a human's skill in the use of available technologies.

In 1976, during the All Volunteer Force, the Armed Services Vocational Aptitude Battery (ASVAB) was introduced. It was used as the single test to be utilized by all military services for both screening and job classification. The ASVAB divided into various subtests and these are:

1. Word Knowledge,
2. Paragraph Comprehension,
3. General Science,
4. Arithmetic Reasoning,
5. Auto & Shop Information,
6. Mathematics Knowledge,
7. Mechanical Comprehension,
8. Electronics Information,
9. Numerical Operations,
10. Coding Speed.

As can be seen the army selection tests have gone from very simple structure to very detailed and technology oriented format with more stress on general problem solving capabilities in a reasonable amount of time (the above list clearly includes three technology sub-areas).

Based on this development we are suggesting the implementation of a new mental test, which will represent the fifth period for future combats. In this new test military forces could be able to identify capabilities of the applicants as well as locate them on a suitable job. We think that the parameters measured in this test would be (in addition to the old ones):

1. Technology adaptation: This is a key area to be tested. If a soldier is unable to adapt to a changing technological scenario, he or she will be at a clear disadvantage in the use and control of robotic technologies.
2. Computer knowledge: The ability to handle artificially intelligent entities is deeply rooted in the ability to deal with computers in general and a facility and skill in using various software tools.
3. Rudimentary understanding of human, animal and machine intelligence: The current generation of tests does measure the intelligence of humans but it is also important for a soldier or police officer now to understand the nature of intelligence and the various paradigms available to implement this in machines.

Future soldiers will work in very different environments that may include fighting with, or against robots either in peace time or during wars. Third world countries may not have the financial resources to buy this new technology, but they certainly can train their human forces with psychological conditioning and simulated games. These training method and tests will not only be applicable to soldiers but also to the police forces. Terrorist associations could use these high-tech robots to cause harm, even in peaceful times and such police training would prove useful in these times.

Conclusions and Recommendations

We have discussed the possibility of robot - human encounter in the battlefield and the problems associated with it including the role of psychological testing. We have pointed out that simulated games can be an effective tool in teaching armies or police forces of the third world countries in dealing with such situations. We feel that there is a clear need for new mental tests as described in this paper, suitable for future military operations. With these new tests military forces may be able to identify capabilities and limitations of the applicants in encounters with artificially intelligent entities or robots. We think that the parameters measured here may be used in assigning them various roles in the battlefield.

In short we recommend:

1. New psychological tests meant to test capabilities and limitations of military men in encounters with artificially intelligent entities.
2. Simulated games for police and military training.

Acknowledgment

This paper is based on an invited talk given by one of us (MAY) at Tec de Monterrey ITESM Campus Santa Fe in April 2003. The authors would like to thank Jose Nicolas Ponciano Guzman, the coordinator of the Masters program for his hospitality at the Department of Mechanical Engineering, Institute Technologic de Morelia, where part of this work was completed.

REFERENCES

[1] "Computerized Personality," Popular Mechanics (September 2000), *<http://popularmechanics.com/science/robotics/>.*

[2] Erik J.F. Canton, Henri L.F. de Groot, and Richard Nahuis," Vested Interests and Resistance to Technology Adoption," *<http://citeseer.ni.nec.com/437919.html>.*

[3] Lawrence C. Kolb, 9a. ed, Modern Clinical Psychiatry.

[4] Anxiety and Stree Disorders Clinic, Ohio State University, *http://anxietv.psv.ohio-state.edu/informat.htm*

[5] E.O. Wheeler, P.D. White, E.W. Reed, and M.E. Cohen, Neurocirculatory Asthenia, JAMA 142:878-889, 1950.

[6] Sun Tzu, "The Art of War - The Oldest Military Treatise In The World," translated from the Chinese introduction and critical with cotes by Lionel Giles, Published M.A. First in 1910, *<http://www.clas.ufl.edu/users/qthursbv/taoism/suntext.htm>* .

[7] Thomas G. Sticht and William B. Armstrong, "Adult Literacy In The United States - A Compendium Of Quantitative Data And Interpretive Comments," *<http://www.nald.ca/fulitext/adlitUS/cover.htm >.*

[8] Joseph Zeidner and Arthur J. Drucker (1988). Behavioral Science in the Army: A Corporate History of the Army Research Institute (Alexandria, VA: U.S. Army Research Institute for the Behavioral and Social Sciences).

[9] "Diagnostic and Statistical Manual of Mental Disorders" 4ed. de., rev. Washington, D.C., American Psychiatric Association, 1995.

[10] Stam R., Akkerman, L.M.A., Wiegant V.M.: Trauma and the gut: interactions between stressful experience and intestinal function. Gut 1997; 40: 704-709

[11] Fass R., Kagan B., Fullerton S., Mayer E.A.: The prevalence of functional gastrointestinal symptoms in male patients with posttraumatic stress disorder (abstract). Gastroenterology 1995; 108: A 597

[12] M.I. Hidalgo, "Transtornos por estres postraumatico," Monograffas de Psiquiatrfa, Num. 03-2001, <*http://www.grupoaulamedica.com/*>.

[13] Joseph Zeidner and Arthur J. Drucker (1983), "Behavioral Science in the Army: A Corporate History of the Army Research Institute," Alexandria, VA: U.S. Army Research Institute for the Behavioral and Social Sciences.

[14] Milton Mater and W. Sims (1986, July). The ASVAB Score Scales: 1980 and World War II. CNR 116.

[15] Brian Waters, Jeffery Barnes, Paul Foley, Stephen Steinhaus and Dianne Brown (1988, October), "Estimating the Reading Skills of Military Applicants: Development of an ASVAB to RGL Conversion Table," HumRRO Final Report 88-22, FR-PRD-88-22 Alexandria, VA: Human Resources Research Organization.

6

ROBOTS OF THE FUTURE BATTLEFIELD

"Military robotic systems will proliferate throughout the 21st century force structure, performing dirty, dangerous, and dull task, while providing a revolutionary capability across the spectru of missions and conflicts."[1]

The future battlefield will be inhabited by a growing number and kind of robots (autonomous mobile physical agents). Successful and efficient application of robots will require a continuously increasing level of coordination, and cooperation. For this reason robots should have new, advanced information capabilities. We summarize the main characteristics of robots of the future battlefield, and demonstrate the necessity of cooperation. Then we analyze the required information capabilities. Finally we discuss the role of semantic interoperability, and the way to achieve it.

Introduction

It can be easily foreseen, that the future battlefield will be inhabited by a growing number and kind of robots (autonomous mobile physical agents). Unmanned aerial, ground, etc. Vehicles carrying different sensors will be used to gather necessary intelligence and information. Other robots will perform different combat tasks: strike targets, jam electronic systems, or construct obstacles. Finally logistic robots will support maneuver units carrying out transportation tasks on the battlefield.

Successful and efficient application) of robots requires a continuously increasing level of coordination, and cooperation. Robots with small "footprint" can cooperate to fulfil tasks far beyond their individual capabilities. It is clear, that not only similar robots, but robots with different functions and capabilities should and will take part in such a cooperation. Successful cooperation requires well-defined information capabilities, e.g. interoperable communication, shared situational awareness, and cooperative planning capabilities.

Robots with the information capabilities mentioned before, will work in a heterogeneous military information environment. They have to exchange information with other robots (or human beings!) not only in a technically, and syntactically, but in a semantically interoperable way. Semantic interoperability is a mutual capability of different actors to develop a common interpretation of identical things (environmental effects, messages, data), sufficiently identical for successful cooperation.

Robots on the battlefield, their future characteristics, necessity of cooperation

The characteristics of military conflicts and threats have dramatically changed. The requirements for cuts in defence budgets lead to the reduction of personnel in almost all NATO-partner countries, and armies. At the same time casualties in out-of-area missions become even more difficult to be politically justified. So substitution of personnel in hazardous environments and during fatigue activities became an important military requirement.

Robots - in general - are machines or devices that work automatically or operated by remote control. In military application unmanned systems are mobile and stationary military systems without a human operator aboard. Main categories of unmanned systems are: unmanned ground vehicles (UGVs), unmanned aerial vehicles (UA Vs), unmanned underwater vehicles (UUVs), unattended munitions (UUVs), and unattended ground sensors (UGSs).

Potential unmanned ground vehicle applications in land combat operations include detection, neutralization, and breaching of mine fields and other obstacles; reconnaissance, surveillance and target acquisition; unexploded ordnance clearance; explosive ordnance disposal; force protection; physical security; fire-fighting; urban warfare; weapons employment; and operations in contaminated and other denied areas. Peacetime applications include the use of small, man-portable systems for earthquake search and rescue, and law enforcement operations.[3] Other possible application is transportation on the battlefield.

Different types of UGVs planned to play different role in combat. Soldier UGVs carried by one or more soldiers perform a variety of tasks (reconnaissance, surveillance, door breach, smoke generation, etc.) in support of dismounted soldiers. Transport (mule) UGVs towed to the operational area by a larger vehicle perform transportation missions (dismounted troop material services, or supplies movement). Armed reconnaissance vehicle UGVs perform armed RST A missions and are capable of manin-the-Ioop weapon fire via a C41SR network. Finally unmanned ground combat vehicles (UGCVs) include robotic direct fire, and robotic non-line-of-sight fire weapon systems.

Unmanned air vehicles will have different types too. Existing UA Vs are principally used to accomplish RSTA missions. Unmanned combat air vehicles (UCAVs), and unmanned combat armed rotorcrafts (UCARs) will augment a force on high risk, high priority missions. UCA Vs, and DCARs will perform: new combat missions that do not currently exist; high-risk missions where the risk to the human life is unwarranted; or current missions where its use is more cost effective than current platforms.

As an example, the US Army's Future Combat Systems (PCS) program seeks to develop concepts of a network-centric, distributed force that includes manned command and control elements (personnel carriers), robotic direct-fire systems, robotic non-lineof-sight (NLOS) weapon systems and all-weather robotic sensor system coupled with other layered sensors.

An FCS unit cell (an ensemble system) will have both manned and unmanned elements, where the robotic elements maneuver together with manned elements in a tactically intelligent manner.

It is almost obvious that future combat will require multiple layers of interactions between warfighters and the autonomous and semi-autonomous systems that will be an indispensable part of the future force, but by all means there will be robots working autonomously on the battlefield. Co-existence, co-working of robots in the same environment is theoretically possible:

- without any knowledge of each other;
- with perception of each other;
- with communication between them;
- and with coordination between them.Teams of robots generally can accomplish tasks more quickly and

> effectively than a single agent working independently on a task. So effective and reliable coordination, cooperation has been and will continue to be an essential element in the success of combat missions with both unmanned and manned assets. Cooperative operations require the ability of two or more robots (unmanned systems) to share data, coordinate their maneuver, and perform tasks synergistically. Cooperative robotics is a modern research field, with applications to such areas where a population of cooperative robots can accomplish tasks that would be difficult, if not impossible for a single robot. Cooperative robotics can use a lot of results from multiagent systems researches (distributed planning, task allocation, communication languages and coordination mechanisms, etc.).

As it is discussed in detail in a research paper prepared for DARPA, there are a variety of methods to approaching the robot coordination problem. Coordination architectures (general forms, by which communication and successive member interactions are performed) are of key importance to robotic workforces, because they considerably influence the synergistic effects of cooperation. The possible architectures include the following:

- centralized coordination ("master-slaves");
- hierarchical coordination ("organizations");
- reactive coordination ("swarms");
- decentralized coordination ("partners").

In case of centralized coordination ("let some 'omniscient' master dictate") a central robot has knowledge of the given requirements, collects all perceived data from the other robots, processes data to find a "solution", then the solution is sent to the robots for execution. In case of hierarchical coordination ("think through the situation fully at various levels, then respond") a planner robot divides an overall task into subtasks, assigns subtasks to other robots, they create (sub)plans, planner resolves conflicts and allows others to proceed. In case of reactive coordination ("directly respond to the stimulus") all robots created equal, they have simple reflex (stimulus-response) rules, that hopefully lead to cooperative behaviour, lack of internal state. Decentralized coordination based also on robots considered equal, but these robots have ability to communicate in some way with their peers, any of them may initiate contact with any other.

Finally the participants of a given (robot-)cooperation can be: homogeneous robots (with identical capabilities); or heterogeneous robots (with specialized capabilities). Analyzing the possible application areas both versions seem to be possible. Ordnance clearance, disposal or physical security (e.g. intrusion detection) are examples for tasks suitable for a homogeneous group of robots, and RST A or combat missions require cooperation of different kinds of robots.

From the considerations discussed previously we can expect a likely scenario where dynamically changing groups of heterogeneous robots with changing capabilities cooperate with each other and with human actors to fulfil common goals by coordinated actions.

Required information capabilities, shared situational awareness, cooperative planning

The necessity of information capabilities for robots is based on their definition. To operate autonomously requires at least information storing and processing capabilities, otherwise operation by remote control requires information communication and transformation capabilities. Information capabilities of robots can be grouped into individual, and group/team capabilities.

Individual information capabilities of robots include: information gathering about relevant aspects of the environment, and about the other actors (human beings and robots) in this environment; communication capabilities to transfer and receive descriptive and prescriptive information to and from other actors; and information processing capabilities to be able to convert sensory data to perception, to do forecasts, and to develop plans. Additionally group (team) information capabilities of robots include the following: interoperable communication; shared situational awareness; cooperative planning.

In psychology and cognitive sciences, situational awareness is considered as knowledge created through interaction between an agent and its environment. In this sense, awareness can be simply defined as "knowing what is ,going on". Basic characteristics of awareness, setting it apart from other kinds of knowing, are the following:

- awareness is knowledge about the state of the same environment bounded in time and space;
- environments change over time, so awareness is knowledge that must be maintained and kept up-to-date: depending on the rate of changes, information has to be continually gathered and updated;
- maintenance of awareness is accomplished through interaction with the environment (gathering information through sensory perception, and actively exploring surroundings based on the information picked up);
- awareness is almost always part of some other activity that is maintaining awareness and is rarely the primary goal of the activity.

A wareness is an everyday phenomenon, and its role becomes more noticeable as situations and environments become more dynamic, complex, information demanding, and with higher workload, or risks.

Creation and maintenance of situational awareness is a three-stage process, with the following components:

- perception of relevant elements of the environment;
- comprehension of those elements;
- prediction of the states of those elements in the near future.

So an agent acting in an environment should first gather perceivable (observable) information; selectively attend to those elements that are most relevant for the task at hand; integrate the incoming perceptual information with existing knowledge and make sense of them in light of the current situation; and finally should be able to anticipate changes in the environment and predict how incoming information will change.

Shared situational awareness is a prerequisite of cooperation, a coordinated, continuously harmonized system of individual situational awarenesses, that in the case of complex groups of actors, can be even multilevel. Situational awareness of individual robots - according to the level and contents of cooperation between them - can overlap each other: to effectively, and successfully accomplish the related activities, they must have identical, or equivalent knowledge of the affected elements of the situation. In addition to these overlaps, naturally any robot's situational awareness can also contain other pieces of knowledge, typical for, and necessary to, the given robot.

To develop a plan for a group .of robots it is necessary to know: what robots are available; and what are the actual capabilities of these robots. In case of dynamically changing groups of robots with changing capabilities it is necessary to manage: joining and leaving of groups; and advertisements of actual capabilities. This is also true for such a group of robots where all of them are of the same type (e.g. robotic jammers), because in a real environment some of them may be destroyed, and/or some of their individual capabilities may have been lost. Of course it should be emphasized that solving these problems is not enough alone to build a cooperative planning system.

In a dynamic and heterogeneous environment of robots to enable successful cooperation all of them have to signal their presence, and to advertise (if necessary to withdraw) their actual capabilities. At the same time others - at least robots with planning tasks - have to seek for given, available capabilities. For efficient handling the available robots, and their actual capabilities in the field of multiagent systems a special class of software-agents are used. Brokers, and matchmakers support matchmaking implementing a publish-subscribe architecture.

It is worth to highlight that both shared situational awareness, and capability matchmaking requires exchange of information in a meaningful, semantically interoperable way. So cooperating robots should have a (partially) common model of the "world" (objects, properties, and relations), and a common model of possible capabilities (services), and their attributes.

Exchange of information in a heterogeneous environment, semantic interoperability

Exchange of information is actually exchange of meaning. The concept of meaning originally connected to human beings, but it can, even should be interpreted in case of systems (robots) as intended meaning, planned interpretation. Information exchange has a commonly accepted three-level model. The first is the physical (material) level of media used; the second is the syntactic level of languages, message and data formats used; and the third is the semantic level of content, and meaning to exchange. NATO common interoperability standards system identifies the three levels as technical, procedural, and operational, and groups interoperability standards according to these categories.

In our days interoperability between cooperating systems (e.g. robots) on the two first levels can be realized easily. The degree of heterogeneity at these levels has significantly decreased, and expected to decrease in the future. Both physical transmission means, and message formats have dominated by standardized solutions. Much more difficult to ensure common interpretation (semantic interoperability) of data transmitted in messages, and functions, services provided by different systems.

In case of military robots, unmanned systems the problem of semantic interoperability, therefore the necessity of the appropriate information capabilities haven't yet really arisen. One of the first appearances of a partial solution of this question can be seen in the case of unmanned aerial vehicles. At the end of 2002 started the formal ratification process of ST ANAG 4586, entitled "Standard Interface of the Unmanned Control System (UCS) for NATO UAV Interoperability". Up to this point, each UAV system has had a different ground control station (GCS), producing systems that use unique elements that employ proprietary protocols and message formats. This hindered interoperability and obstructed widespread dissemination of payload data/information. Operation of multiple types of air vehicles from the same GCS has not been possible. Implementation of ST ANAG 4586 will enable information between different VA Vs to be collated and shared via common ground stations.

In case of unmanned combat aerial vehicles (UCA Vs) the necessity of information, and semnantical interoperability between military robots is expressed in the format of a technical requirement called network connectivity: a dynamically managed, interoperable, high-capacity connectivity between UCA Vs, manned aircrafts, UA Vs, off-board sensors, and ground stations. Cooperative engagement capability and development of a single integrated air picture requires cooperative inter-platform operations, meaningful information exchange.

In the development concepts of Future Combat Systems there is an abstraction layer that insulate C41SR applications from low level details of the C41SR sensor packages. This layer (C4ISR Sensor Data Management) provides sensor control services, manages the publishing of sensor data within platforms and to the FCS network in an FCS standard sensor data format, and provides a gateway to external sensor data sources from other (unit of employment, joint, national, and coalition) assets.

Future military forces ("hybrid armies") will have a lot of robot components that will play an essential role in almost all military functions and activities. Military robots will fulfill their tasks mainly in cooperation with other robots and human actors. The cooperative robot-robot, and human-robot groups will be dynamically changing, and heterogeneous in many respect.

Military robots must have appropriate ("value-added", "enabler") information capabilities, and these capabilities will significantly determine their usefulness. One of the most important capabilities will be the capability to support semantic interoperability, a prerequisite of meaningful information exchange in a dynamically changing group of possibly more or less heterogeneous robots.

7

FUTURE OF ROBOTIC WARFARE

Nearly every country in the world has Unmanned Aerial Vehicle programs in development, this means our allies and our enemies. We have even seen technology leak from friendly countries to questionable ones and then end up in the hands of International Terrorists. Just recently Hezbolla has bagged about Hying a Unmanned Aerial Vehicle into Northern Israel. No one understands what the purpose in doing this is. But it stands to reason that if they are strapping bombs on down syndroe kids and sending them into Israel to get on buses and blow themselves and everyone else up. That you cannot put anything passed them? Is Hezbolla planning single mission Unmanned Aerial Vehicle model airplane kamikaze attacks? It appears so. As these international Terrorists get more sophisticated with their weaponry, we will have to find ways to defeat these Unmanned Aerial Vehicles and do so in a way. Which does not give away our troops positions. Think about it.

Enemy UAV Defense is underconsideration

Unmanned Aerial Vehicles should be shot down from the air rather than the ground because if they are Hown tele-robotically the operator who is looking down and forward will not know where the anti-aircraft device is. If the enemy uses UmnannedAerial Vehicles to draw fire, which is a smart move for them, then once fired upon the Unmanned Aerial Vehicle whether it is shot down or not has now located our weaponry and troops. Likewise if we have a loitering Unmanned Aerial Vehicle above the enemy once they shoot it, we see the hostile fire and either "hell fire missile it" or take coordinates of the insurgents locations and wire it to the most appropriate component of the net-centric blue force.

If an enemy Unmanned Aerial Vehicle locates our troops it is only a matter of time before they are eliminated, so it is essential to shoot down all enemy robotic or autonomous, AI or not, Unmanned Aerial Vehicles. Shooting down a Unmanned Aerial Vehicle with small arms fire is dangerous and nearly impossible. It is for that reason that they must be shot down from the air. It is easier to shoot one down from the air, but not an easy over all task. The best way to shoot them down would be aerial laser from a floating reflector above the battles space or just above line of sight. The Unmanned Aerial Vehicle will not know where it came from, it will fry the electronics immediately and do so at the speed of light. By using an aerial blimp we have additional coordinates in the 3D battles pace. Shooting down swam is of incoming Unmanned Aerial Vehicles should deploy similar tactics for best results (eliminating all Unmanned Aerial Vehicles MAVs in the swann).

Educating Yourself on Unmanned Vehicles and the Future Fighting Force

Many ann chair couch potato Generals sit and scream at the TV when it comes to fighting wars. Convenient indeed, sitting their calling the shots and complaining about what is going on at the unit or ground level - how on Earth would they know what is going on, as whatever is on the TV is hardly real.

Information seems to be power and therefore, I must recommend that those who wish to educate themselves on the US war efforts learn a little bit about Unmanned Vehicles and the Future Fighting Force. Where can you learn more? Well there are many sources which provide me with information and allow the intake needed to prepare a paper in 2-days off the top of my head about the subject.

The Internet has been a wonderful tool and the many online newsletters in Robotics, Unmanned Vehicles, Artificial Intelligence, Defense Topics, Space, Automotive, Tanking, Communication, Materials and Bleeding Edge Research are immensely valuable. Other good sources of reality based information include all the digital online libraries at the major Universities for sharing their knowledge.

Consider all the magazines on the subject and information in Aviation Week and Space Technologies, Space Daily Express and the top Defense Magazines. Of course first you ought to read the US Army's Future Fighting Force Roadmaps and reports to Congress. They are put out each year along with those from the US Air Force Research Lab and the US Navy.

Perhaps if you really want to learn more, check out the DARPA Robotic Unmanned Vehicles Competitions that propel this area of science. That ought to give one a start in learning all about the future of Unmanned Vehicles in the modern battlespace.

Indeed, even if war is something you do not wish to think about, I see a tremendous future potential with the transfer technologies for Tncking, Transportation, Policing, Border Patrol and preventing auto accidents. The DARPA Team and their public relations efforts, contests and hospitality has been nothing short of a class act. These efforts help to bring forth a new generation of engineers focused on the unmanned ground vehicle mission. All in all, it's all good.

Unmanned Vehicles and Future Rules of Engagement

The idea of robots sent to annihilate the enemy is troubling for many to contemplate, especially after watching some of the Hollywood Movies of the last couple decades. Some ask what if they mal-function, yet could it really be any worse than human soldiers who in the past have raped and pillaged? It is a fact of war, in past periods it was accepted, the spoils of war, today it is not acceptable, but it happens. Will robots left to their own recognizance be any less problematic with their rules of engagement?

Indeed one has to ask if one side uses robots, as whose to say the other side will have as sophisticated of robots which will have better artificial intelligent software able to discern friendly, non-combatant, enemy or foe? Who makes this decision and who is designing these systems and programming their software? If the systems are damaged who is to say if that malfunction may cause unnecessary death of civilians or initiate friendly fire?

The question with robotic war fighters has been pondered: Who decides who lives or dies? Whether this question is answered soon or whether it takes time to render such a decision, the predicament and perplexing problem is here and it is here now.

Few would argue that international terrorists should be eliminated and by any and all means possible including robots or UAVs with Hell-Fire Missile Systems. There have already been high-ranking military men and futurist philosophers contemplate this problem and the consensus appears to be that Robots should not be allowed to kill humans unless a human being is in the loop, which seems to point towards the future of "Video Game Warfare" thru a tele-robotic motif. Then the robotic unmanned ground vehicle, system or UA V is nothing more than a tool at the hand of a human?

2007 Trendsin UAVs (Unmanned Aerial Vehicles)

Unmanned Aerial Vehicles or UAV s have proved themselves worth their weight in gold in the military. Today Unmanned Aerial Vehicles can be flown tele-robotically and controlled from a distance by a pilot on the ground. Some UAVs can fly completely autonomously once launched. Unmanned Aerial Vehicles make a perfect surveillance tools in the modern net centric battle space. With many high-tech electronic sensors they can pick up the enemy via infrared on a pitch-black night.

There have been instances where UAVs have fired upon enemy targets using huffier missiles and destroy the target. There have been situations where the ground control link was lost on a tele-robotically flown UAV and the Unmanned Aerial Vehicle returned its self to the airport and landed safely, The technology advances in unmanned robotic vehicles has come a long way in the last decade and this trend will continue.

What will the future of UAVs bring? Well, we are witnessing the miniaturization of UAVs as the sensors and electronics get smaller and more robust Currently the United States military is using Micro Air Vehicles or MAVs that are the size of a small bird, Current technology trends predict that the top universities in the United States will perfect insect size MAVs. Meanwhile, The Air Force Research Laboratory has put out a roadmap calling for unmanned fighter aircraft and attack aircraft in the near future. We can also expect cargo aircraft UAVs.

With the rapid advancement of artificial intelligence it appears that the fighter pilot's days are numbered and soon human pilots will no longer rule the skies. You can also expect transfer technologies to be handed down into many commercial applications. I hope you will enjoy this book and discussion of all these topics and more, as we look at the future of UA Vs for both the military and private sector.

I appreciate your mind's bandwidth on this topic, as UAVs are not only here to stay, but will be a big part of future aviation history. And you need to be thinking here. Perhaps this article is of interest to propel thought in 2007?

2007 Trends in Artificial Intelligent UAV Fighter Aircraft

The Future of the Top Gun Fighter Pilot is almost over and indeed their days are numbered. This will be the last generation of human fighter pilots due to the rapidly advancing artificial intelligence and Unmanned aerial vehicle technologies. Soon airliners will fly themselves just like light-rail systems only without the tracks. The cost savings to build aircraft without cockpits and human systems for control will save hundreds of thousands of dollars or even millions in some cases. But this is not the only reason.

Consider if you will the cost of the military to recruit, train, house, feed a human fighter pilot. Think about the loss if you lose them in battle, not only have you lost a 50 million dollar or more aircraft, you have lost all your return on investment in training too. Indeed human pilots also have limits that future artificial intelligent unmanned aerial vehicles will not have. Humans cannot withstand much more than 8 '08 and we have missiles that can handle over 18 'Gs now. In the future Fighter Aircraft without humans will be able to do the same and therefore complete nearly impossible maneuvers by today's standards.

The current predictions and UAV Unmanned Aerial Vehicle Roadmaps of the United States Air Force and United States Navy are calling for increased use of robotic aircraft and huge decreases in human piloted aircraft Both cost and technology are driving this progression, but also driving this solution is the competition or potential adversaries. For our fighter aircraft to be more competitive and continue to dominate the skies removing the weakest link. The human pilot makes a lot of sense much to the chagrin of pilots like my Dad who did 250 combat missions in Vietnam in an US Navy A-4.

I hope you will enjoy this intellectual thought and concept. Maybe you will find it mindful and thought provoking, as this is its intended purpose. Perhaps this article is of interest to propel thought?

The Inventor Entrepreneur Must Risk Crash and Burn Scenarios to Push the Envelope on Science

If you really want to be an inventor sometimes you have to mortgage your house, beg, borrow or steal in order to set your project in motion. Still even the best garagc inventors often crash and burn. How would I know? Well I often talk with such inventors, innovators and forward thinkers on a daily basis. In fact as a retired entrepreneur I have even used some of my own cash on some rather interesting projects, which yes, you guessed; Crashed and Burned.

Indeed, I built a little UAV Unmanned Aerial Vehicle or MAV rather, a Micro-Air Vehicle. Spent about $200 bucks in parts to make a flying beer can? Hey, don't laugh, I could have made a fortune if I was hired for a Super Bowl Commercial, may be even made 1000% return on investment. Unfortunately that is not how the story ends? It crashed and burned, actually worse.

The little unit has a polymer type muscle for the wings. Once it gets going it goes for a while without any help. I had designed a little MAV bird figuring the right Reynolds number it would flap a polymer wing. I built a Soda Can model and flew it out of an industrial park and I lost it, as it flew over a building and a wall and crashed on the Fwy, was run over into pieces, ah heck any way.

Darn thing was too much work, but it flew actually had a lot of power, but very little stability and would have made an interesting decoy tool for the USMC or something') I certainly hope this article is of interest and that is has propelled thought. The goal is simple; to help you in your quest to be the best in 2007. I thank you for reading my many articles on diverse subjects, which interest you.

High Tech: NovTel GPS

The NovTel GPS system is definitely something to talk about and indeed becoming quite famous as it just happened to be the GPS system riding on board of Stanford University's Volkswagon which just happen to win the DARPA Grand Challenge and the 2-million dollar cash prize. If you will recall the DARPA Grand Challenge had over 50 challengers driving vehicles through desert course almost 200-miles long, without any driver.

The UGV Unmanned Ground Vehicle nicknamed "Stanley" averaged 19.1 miles per hour that day. Stanley completed the race with the NovAtel's Propak(R)LBplus with Omnistar HP Service for precise positioning data aboard. It worked better than all the others including super star Grad students from such notable Universities as Cal-rech, Berkeley, Virigina Tech, Georgia Tech, MIT and Carnegie Mellon all known for their robust robotic prowess.

The NovTel Propak GPS receiver coupled with the OmniSTAR L-band signals was able to correct its movements while it drove through the tough course. The accuracy is said to be within such tight tolerances that their was no competition at that point. The system even was able to make quick transitions while coming from GPS blackouts in tunnels, without error. The winning combination is something to talk about and the NovTel Propak is indeed the system of choice and the race for robotic warfare continues.

The X-50A Dragonfly Having Trouble in Development

Imagine an unmanned aerial vehicle UAV, which can take off vertically and hover and then stopped its rotor blades and then fly forward like an airplane? Indeed, the Boeing Co. has built such aircraft and this UAV is perfect for the new Net-centric Battlespace. It is capable of surveillance in real-time and can be operated off of the ship or without a runway. Its range is suitable to protect United States troops and soldiers in hostile territories and alert them of any potential threat approaching.

Unfortunately, such a revolutionary design in aerospace technology is not without its problems in and the prototype of the X-50A Dragonfly has crashed into was destroyed at the Yuma proving grounds for United States military. This is a special project with DARPA and if this aircraft ever makes it to the front lines it could prove to be a valuable asset indeed. Since all the prototypes have now been destroyed in crashes it is hard to say if the project can continue. However, all the data and research, which went into the project is invaluable. And may definitely come in quite useful for future projects.

The hardest part of stich a design is the transition from hovering or vertical flight to forward flight. One thought, is to allow the transition period to include departure flight recovery during the complex manoeuvre. The X-50A is designed to fly at 120 miles per hour with the rotor blades spinning and then stop the rotor blades and ride out the transition into forward flight, allowing for very high speeds. The concept is good and the tests should continue however I believe we need a little redesigning and have posted my ideas at an online think tank site. Consider all this in 2006.

Abandoned Anchor Retrieval RFID System

There will be times when an anchored ship in the US Military needs to move fast and go after a rapidly increasing situation and task which must be accomplished immediately. If the anchors are deployed then they need a capacity to drop the rest of the chain and leave the anchor there. With a backup anchor on-board.

The anchor, which is left will be fitted with an RFID homing tracking device and it can be retrieved at a later date by specially fitted UUV underwater unmanned vehicle. The UUV will pick up the chain via a cable it attaches and bring that cable up to the ship which will then hoist the cable and anchor chain up until which time the actual anchor clears the ocean bottom.

Perhaps a study should be to determine how much time could be saved if the anchor system retrieval was not an issue? Could the ship, which was already mining, move fast and be gone saving ten minutes or more? If so, ten minutes in a high stress situation could be of major value indeed.

There may be other uses for this technology for other vessels and uses and an RFID retrieval system makes sense for anyone involved in UUV or ROVs also. In fact there are many ways this technology can be used for other things that can also become a huge concern. So we need to be thinking here and consider all this in 2006.

Organic Decoy Devices for Warfare (ODDW)

We can genetically modify a rat to be the same body temperature as a humans, then parachute in several thousand rats into enemy territory. These rats will pick up the enemies advanced warning and intension sensors by way of heat signature.

The enemy, thus thinks they are a division of troops with heavy armament trying to hide, perhaps interpreting these signatures as thousands of troops with all but a little of their skin showing. Think of the Predator movie where Sylvester Stallone was being hunted by the alien for sport.

When "Sly" covered his skin with thick mud only a little heat signature could be seen. Troops with heavy bulletproof vests made of Kevlar with ceramic peck plates and helmets would appear similar and thus the area of a rat would be a similar amount of heat signature of human wearing such gear. Once you fool the enemy you can capture him?

Seeing thousands of such heat signatures would mimic what the enemy expects to see when they see thousands of troops in a battalion of infantry. The enemy thus would get scared and prepare to defend against the perceived imminent invasion. As the enemy gets scared and advances on the threat of an invading force of decoy rats we monitor and wait for enemy to fire on thousands of rats, then quickly mark the location from which the incoming fire, ordinance and missiles are launched. Once the enemy gives away their defense positions we send in the first round of UAVs with lethal weapons. EA (electronic attack) devices and smart munitions.

This idea has been perpetuating itself from news events such as the problem with the thousands of rats in Mexico town, which survived their own poisoning when the poison killed all the cats which were controlling their populations. Also Sandia's all new Sarge robotic territorial guarding unmanned vehicle (ATV with heat signature and machine guns). The movie with the Arnold Swarznegger "The Governator" with the flying UAVs in the latest terminator genre also played a part in this thought. The Border Patrol, Coast Guard and Military use of the predator UAVs and use of sensors to protect infrastructure also played a part in this concept. All in all it appears that such battlefield techniques appear to be heading us in this direction.

Using the technology against itself and the rats as bait seems to be a great way to save human life during military actions of political will and helps defeat enemy. One might liken such a concept to the Chinese art of Judo using the opponents power to against him or the political definition of Diplomacy, "the art of letting someone else get your way.'

Now then since we can all agree that this idea or concept of using organic decoys makes a lot of sense in the ever-changing battlespace, how do we raise the temperature of rats to mimic that of human beings?

There are several really simple ways to change the heat signature of the rats, even ways to do this without killing them or seriously hurting them. The easiest way without using genetic manipulation and using the KISS Method would be to simply feed them something, which would temporarily increase their body temperatures.

http://www.ncbi.nlm.nih.gov/entrez/query.fcgi? cmd=Retrieve&db= PubMed&list- uids =2309941 &dopt=Abstract,

This might be the best way because as the rats got closer and closer the effect would of the food would wear off and then all of a sudden they would all disappear, thus putting terror and fear into the enemy as they can no longer find the invading forces. Where did they go, did they hide in a cave, go into a tent, which is hiding them from radar? Did they get in a vehicle? Where? Then they might send out a searching recon team, which could be immediately taken out., meaning the must send another to see what happen to them as once they are gone communication will no longer be available.

Meanwhile why they are looking they will be communicating with those in charge whose position is now given away. Such a trick would be aggravating to the enemy because then the signatures would appear and then disappear, meaning, where did they go, meaning enemy must go on high alert and that means more motion and activity from enemy, including communication, movement, fear and action thus giving away information and locations. As this occurs the enemy has one more unknown to deal with prior to the electronic attack as we gather information from the enemy. Our enemy is hesitant, in fear and giving away all of its locations and communication sources.

If we sent the rats in several large boxes which opened with a timer or were the doors of the boxes were made of food themselves, then they would eat themselves out of the box and and then proceed to look for more food. We would time the thickness of the door made of food to when you wanted to launch the attack. As studying the time to eat the door with 1000 rats could be easily studied in advance. By using this thought process therefore the delivery aircraft could fly in under cover of weather or other temporary diversion and return and will be no where near when the rats finally got out of the box. Thus even more baffling to the enemy since there are no support vehicles, aircraft or other devices in the area. Just what appears to be lots of troops without support heading their way.

How do we keep the rats traveling in the direction we wish? Well a couple of ideas here. First lets not forget the story of the dogs used to deliver hand grenades to the enemy. The masters would say go fetch and attack and the dogs would an towards the enemy, but all the gun fire and chaos would scare the dogs and then they would return to their owners? Whoops?

First there are a couple of ways to do this. One is to put a bad smell upwind by way of single mission UAVs, delivering a smell bomb, warning the rats to go the other way. Or put positive smells, generally food up wind so they travel in the direction of food. One way to do this is to use several box drops of food a few days in advance upwind towards the enemy by way of UAV. Or have CIA operatives in country dropping positive smell bombs. Then another box several miles away towards the target again and they would smell it and go to it. And in that box the food would have in it:

Then another box even further away with the ingredients, which cause increased body temps once again. The rats will move, disappear, reappear closer, then disappear and then move and reappear, thus looks like troop movements, which do not exist, perfect decoy?

If we drop off 20,000 rats some with electronic pulse devices strapped on them in 20 different locations we can over whelm the enemy, wake up the communication and start movement and then attack after just prior to the coordinated attack we send our an electronic attack to kill the communication and electronics of the enemy. All targets are found and locked, game over. RATS'D. Recon Animal Territorial Sensor Decoys.

Robots to Fight Future Wars

Abstractly speaking the new unmanned vehicle robotic technologies, both UGVs and UAVs currently under development will change the future of warfare. Today there are discussions on the ethical implications of this changing paradigm along with the new strategies, surveillance tactics and future innovation that will be implemented. Being considered also are the political and media related issues.

The game of hide and seek, electronic attack and robots VS humans and/or robots VS robots are projected into the future in these dialogues as military men, philosophers and diplomats alike contemplate the realities on the road. The future cometh in the modern battles pace - those participating must: A.dapt or Die.

What Types of robotic systems are we talking about? Well when we discuss robots in warfare, we are talking about Unmanned Vehicles, that is to say unmanned ground and aerial vehicles.

Pahaps you have heard about these, they go by names such as: UAV, UCA V, UGV, UUV and they are controlled either by telerobotics, or autonomously. These robots are the future of warfare.

The United States Military is not alone in such tools of war. Robots in human conflict are at home in many nations military. Countries like India, Russia, China, Iran, UK, Germany, France, Italy, Israel and Australia all have UAV programs.

Of course so does Al Qaeda, Hezbollah, Syria and many of the other International Terrorist groups. Luckily those who plot against us and free peoples of the world do not have the sophistication that our systems do, but nevertheless, they do have access to these tools of war.

Directing Lightning to Enemy Combatants

Is it possible to use Lightning Storms to hit our enemies in the battles pace during wartime? Owning the weather, which is a military directive and absolute goal by 2025, maybe the key to getting our enemies to serve our political will. Imagine creating a lightning Thunder Storm over your enemy area, one which disrupt their radar guided weapons? Then directing any built up energy in the clouds from the friction of the storms into lightning bolts onto communication towers. Command and control centers or even to strike convoys, tanks, aircraft or Unmanned Aerial or Ground Vehicles. (UAV or UGV)

There are many ways to send a charge to via microwave, laser or directed sound waves to build up a static charge on an object making it inviting for a potential lightning strike. Sounds good right, well as long as you are not on the receiving end of 100,000 to million volts of energy travelling at the speed of light into your base camp, command center or military vehicle, in that case no, it is not so great really.

If we can use lightning to take out our enemies, combatants or those who wish us ill then in fact we will have less of those sorts of people trying to attack us. Plus we can reduce collateral damage and not have the environment problems of exploded ordinance after wards, just a lot of fried electronic equipment and enemies who have simply given up their will to fight and promise to behave now. Think on this, we are.

Net-centric Data Storage Using Marine Robotic Equipment

Using Mechanical Fish as Repeater Stations and Data Storage for information to complete OODA Loop and eliminate the issues of bandwidth problems in net-centric warfare. Mechanical fish are easy enough to build;

- http://www.egr.msu.edu/~memaste7/proto1.htm
- http://www.egr.msu.edu/~memaste7/fish.htm
- http://web.mit.edu/towtank/www/pike/
- http://robotics.caltech.edu/~kristi/

We can use these devises to assist us in data collection and since it is mechanical it win not bite on any fishing lines and be equipped with a cutter device to go throw local fishing nets. Provided the fish is large enough no few bigger fish will try to eat it and with razor fins, god help them if they try.

The Net-centric component of the robotic fish can surface to receive data from UGV and Troops, Equipment maintenance data to be retrieved during non-peak usage times. Since we are building mobile cell sites for cellular phones in tanks, on boats and in spherical balloons, putting one inside a mechanical fish, but it would only receive the data and store it in a water proof, terabyte, underwater, fully operational swimming robotic mechanical fish.

Each robotic repeater fish will swim around in a grid pattern to the other repeaters laying down a perfect coverage pattern for marine communication. The military applications arc obvious, but also consider the concept for marine environmental issues, marine communication, oil spill and dumping control and defense of our shore lines?

DOD and DARPA Discussion

September 2005

There is so much bureaucracy in the US Government that one has to wonder if in fact they ever do anything right. Often we will here about some new government program or something good the government is doing, yet we later find out it was pure hokum and Public Relations.

Government's job is to protect the American People, yet we so often see that they are not able to protect us. Most of us are pro-military and the thought that perhaps the military might run a bad as the government is a little unnerving. Has the bureaucracy and political correctness infiltrated the military to the point that it cannot get its job done? We hope not however the DOD's own red tape is an issue in the security of our nation.

Is there a leader amongst us who could do a better job streamlining that BS and mind you I am from a military family and I am 100% in support of the US Military, but as I watch the other branches of our government botch every single endeavour, one must ask the question. Many see so many innovation blocks that they truly worry about the safety of the American people in the future.

The military leadership is fairly arrogant so I doubt they take much of anything in from outside observations and we must also realize without that level of arrogance and self confidence they would not be able to do their jobs, but still if you add in the level of bureaucracy of the rest of the United States Government it is a scary notion. Arrogance and Bureaucracy are a recipe for disaster, similarly incompetence and inefficiency has been the US Government's major hurdle in the past three decades.

Many innovators find that delivering their concepts to military is nearly impossible, yet giving innovations and ideas to their profit motivated contractors gets quick results and they occasionally see such ideas being used. One thing we have seen recently is a new trend where the Advanced Research Division of the Military, DARPA, is actively seeking out innovators and inventors for ideas and concepts to use in the defense of our nation. Recently we see the DARPA Grand Challenge where teams are competing to complete a 200-mile course in the desert with unmanned ground vehicles (UGVs). These teams are indeed some of the brightest amongst us and this technology win assist our military in doing their job, better with less loss of life.

Imagine a UGV hitting a roadside bomb? No loss of life, therefore the International Terrorists have made no progress in propelling their terror. Of course this is only one thing in a long list of new technologies that DARPA is working on to make our Military more efficient perhaps the US Military can move beyond political correctness and bureaucracy and use their intense self-confidence to win battles and protect the American People. Think on this.

2007 Trends in Robotics

Ever consider the Future of Robotics? What will it really be like? Did Science Fiction get it right, if not how close were they? Will robots be everywhere and involved in every aspect of life? Will robots eventually take over all the modern Factories; will robots be making robots too? Which sectors will we see robots excel in? Will we see more;

- Robots in Commerce - Retail, Services, Field,
- Robots in the home - Maids, Washing Car, Doing Chores, Mowing the Lawn,
- Robots in Security - Guards, Guard Dogs, Bomb Sniffers, Bomb Squads,
- Robots to the Rescue - FEMA, Earthquake, Hurricanes, Wild Fires
- Robots for the Weather and Environment - Unmanned Aerial Vehicles
- Robots in Transportation - Light Rail, Cars, Aircraft
- Robots in Distribution Trains, Warehouses
- Robotic Androids—Assistants, Mentors, Educators
- Robots and Artificial Intelligence- Thinking Machines and Systems
- Robots in the Military - Smart Munitions, Net-Centric Systems, UAVs

As you can see from this partial list, this subject; The Future of Robotics indeed warrants a bit of discussion on this subject. The Robots and Robotics of the future will shape our societies and civilizations forever. Are we ready for the runway ahead? Who will design, build, market and repair all these robots and robotic machines? Is our education system up for the challenge to fulfil the future needs in these industries?

Let us contemplate the changes in life style, standard of living and quality of life, as robots do our dirty work, do our jobs and simplify our lives. We must now consider this future, as it is rapidly approaching and has already started, soon it will be; Robots, Robots Everywhere. Please use this book as a thinking exercise and open your mind to the potential eventualities.

I thank you for considering this topic as it is an important subject as we plot a course into a Brave New World. Perhaps this article is of interest to propel thought in 2007

Choosing to Die or Choosing Death by Robot

In the future thru life extension we will be able to choose when we die. There will be miracle drugs, Super Vitamin C and replacement parts such as artificial limbs, hearts, lungs and the latest and greatest robotics. Will be choose to remain 100% human or extend life thru robotic parts, merging with machines? One might choose to go natural, but as we may choose to replace parts and live to see our great, great, great, great grand children if the Earth does not fill up with too many people? Or we may choose for space colonies since there is estimated to be over 30 Billion humans on the planet by 2050.

Will death by robot become a reality? When we replace parts until we are more robot than human and at what point do we cease being human and become something else? Well it is true "choosing to die" does not currently have anything to do with robotics, but it will soon. And soon enough We will cure every disease and delete many of the accidents that happen to humans and be able to "fix them" and stop aging. Many have prophesized this and Ray Kurzweil has a number of followers of his "singularity" concept. If we stop aging them BioTech and or changing parts that we cannot grow for some reason, then well it has everything to do with the future of robotics and the BioTech revolution merger.

Many a studies of humankind agree, that biological evolution has not kept up with the computer age and it is causing issues with our civilizations and societies, no doubt. At the same time the reinvention of society is not able to take the beast out of the human either. And we keep sweeping those innate characteristics under the carpet. Those negative aspects of the human species keep emerging over and over again. They keep popping up where we don't want them and then refuse to address them and we make new laws against them. Sweeping them under the calvet is a real problem as we move into the future period of hyper scientific discovery.

If you were given the choice of going completely 100% human, choosing to die or Choosing Death by Robot, which would you choose? What if being human was considered inferior in the future? Are you afraid of change, caught in religious dogma or are you looking forward to the future? Think on this, as it will not be long now.

Automated Robotic Reciprocal Response Unmanned Ground Vehicles for Urban Battlespace

Currently, The Future Force of the United States Army is developing weapons for the battle space, which will allow them with pinpoint accuracy to know where mortar rounds might hit. There are also new weapons being designed which could tell exactly where a sniper has fired from. By knowing the location of your enemy who is firing upon you, the next logical step is to remove said enemy and the sooner the better.

In the future automated robotic reciprocal response unmanned ground vehicles for the urban battle space will return fire with a devastating force. Those who are dumb enough to fire itpon the US Forces, human or robotic, will be eliminated instantaneously.

In the future unmanned ground vehicles and robotics will rule the battle space and remove enemy insurgents and international terrorists surgically with pinpoint accuracy and little if any ancillary damage. For those that believe they can fight our future fighting forces and the robotics that come with the team; they are in for a big surprise.

Of course these enemies will never be able to tell anybody about this because they will be hit so fast they will not know what it was which took them out. Our men and women in uniform are too important to risk in the battle space against enemy insurgents and international terrorists that most people believe are worth less than a nickel.

2007 Trends in Underwater Robotics

The Underwater World of Robotics is progressing at a record clip. If you look at the military expenditures from the Deep Sea Underwater Coast Guard road maps or the United States Naval Research exploits it is obvious that the technology is moving at break-neck speed. Indeed. We arc watching improved performance in ROVs for underwater rescues, deep sea exploration and underwater infrastructure construction and repair in the private sector also moving forward rapidly.

If you will peruse the engineering research departments of the Top Universities around the world you will see lots of prototypes of Underwater Autonomous Vessels being produced and tested. With a plethora of innovative technologies, capabilities and applications. The number of white papers on the subject has increased by ten-fold over the last decade and a half and the amount of collaboration around the world with these technologies is truly amazing, sharing information and data in real-time.

It is amazing that we are exploring other worlds and planning space colonies and yet we have a huge amount of exploration to do right here under our oceans as well. Indeed. Others have considered this and are doing just that. We are learning more about underwater volcanic vents, finding new species never seen by human eyes and understanding more and more about the oceans ceo-system, landscape, water Hows and seismic activity.

I appreciate your brain power on this subject and do please consider the importance of this topic. The future is hear and it is up to us to decide where to take it next. Perhaps this article is of interest to propel thought in 2007?

2007 Military Tech: Mounting (HEL) High Energy Lasers on Robotic Sentries for Boarder Patrol

It truly is time to stop pussy-footing around and begin to leverage our best technologies to secure our borders. One new advancement in robotics is a Sandia Lab created autonomous vehicle sentry; which looks some what like an ATV, but fully robotic.

I advise that we mount a small compact (HEL) High Energy Laser unit on these robotic sentries for Border Patrol on the US-Mexico Border. Why use a laser? Well because they arc a highly effective weapon and by completely burning the drug dealer or enemy combatant attempting to gain entry into our nation, it will provide a BBQ meal for localized animal species in desert regions where food is scarce. This also saves money in clean up or burials and less paperwork as well.

Since we have these technologies we should be deploying them immediately to protect our nation and this will save millions if not billions of dollars in training of Border Patrol Officers and billions in salary and pensions in the future. If the dog dealers engage the robotic sentries, then they are toast. Literally. And this is a good thing, but also consider those International Terrorists attempting to sneak over the border to become insurgents in our nation. Stopping them and BBQ'ing them prior to entry makes a lot of sense too.

The high-energy laser system could easily be mounted on a on the Sandia Sarge Unit and it would be fully lethal as needed. We must secure the borders of our nation and this is an excellent way to do that. Perhaps you might consider this concept, as they could come in handy in places like Iraq as well in 2007.

Will Future Civilizations Destroy All the Robots We Build?

The robotic revolution is before us and we are having kids in school compete in robotic competitions. Indeed, we are getting an incredible number of new innovations and technologies from all this and these kids once in college and bona fide research facilities will create the next generation of robots.

These robots will help us explore other worlds, they will fly our aircraft and they will make life at home so much easier. They will care for the elderly, take our pets for walks and do the jobs we often do not wish to do. They will drive our tanks, our trains and harvest our food from the Fields. Robots will also be fighting our wars, mining our government and policing our citizens.

There in lies the problem, robots will soon rule our world and we have all seen the sciencefiction movies which depict wars against humans and artificially intelligent robotic androids. Is that truth coming, will that be the reality of the future? Will future civilizations destroy all the robots we build in the present period?

Will future generations curse ours for building these robots? Will they label this era a time when mankind was irresponsible with technology and allowed it to an away and eventually an over society? If this is the case then we ought to be very careful as we move forward and build robots to serve us and not for us to serve them and become a slave race to our own technologies.

Personally I am very proud of our technology and look forward to the robotics of the future, but if you disagree with me I see your point and thus I wrote this article from your perspective not mine.

2006 Predictions for Robotics

Indeed 2005 was the year of the robots, but there arc many more years to come. It cannot be debated that in 2005 the greatest strides in robotics yet was observed. We watched NASA use a robotic arm to assemble things in space. We watched a car named "Stanley" move through the desert averaging nearly 30 miles per hour without a driver, fully autonomously without remote control.

Wall Street applauded iRobot as it mack its public offering debut. We even observed robotic automotive factories and their efficiencies to force 60,000 Union Autoworkers out of their jobs as both GM and Ford announced massive layoffs. But that's not all as scientists realized a dream when a monkey and his brain was hooked up to a computer screen and the monkey moved an object on the screen simply by thought for a free banana, ushering in a new age of the blending of man-computer and robotic machines.

Scientists made robotic fish and the United States Military eenlisted UAVs or Unmanned Aerial Vehicles to help fight the war on terror in 2005. Artificial limbs and prosthetics advanced sharply in 2005 as soliders maimed in battle from roadside IEDs came back and needed body parts.

We will see robotics get very small and the introduction of nanobots in the real world not just in scientific journals and white papers but being produced for all sorts of applications from environmental membrane filtration to medical uses in the body. We will see UAVs, which fly together and work together in teams and swarms. We will see disaster assistance robots, which actually go in and save lives. We will see urban infrastructure surveillance bots and home security robots that look like the family pet.

Along with this we will see the first sex android robots produced and sold in Japan. We will see elderly care robots, multi-use home cleaning robots and robotic transportation such as buses and trucks. All this and more is coming and will be here soon, some may others by the middle of June.

2007 Trends in Artificial Intelligence

Very soon Artificial Intelligence will indeed surpass human intelligence. Very soon the human mind's ability to reason will be left in the dust by artificial intelligence computers and unless the human mind is interfaced with the artificial intelligence brain, humans will never catch up. Artificial Intelligence will be much different than the days of the Old Blue beating the human chess champion, as that was not true Artificial Intelligence; smart enough to beat a human, yes, but Artificial Intelligence, no, not really.

Indeed, artificial intelligent computers will write their own programs as they encounter situations and try different things to achieve a goal. If they fail they will record those mistakes and never make them again, meanwhile they will send this information to all the other artificially intelligent computers linked up so they too will learn net-centrically or them a common collective of computer shared elata. This will mean that every lesson learned gets learned once and passed onto the whole.

Human Brains which are hooked into these systems will find additional abilities and unlimited data available, digital online real time libraries of all the information every collected by machine, as well as humans in the collective. Artificial Intelligent machines will be commonplace; metacentric cars, aircraft, home appliances, entertainment devices, military defense and health care to fix broken humans. Of course the high tech world with the use of these machines in everything from robotics to space applications will move at light speed due to the incredible efficiency of real-time collaboration.

Discoveries in Artificial Intelligence may become the single greatest achievement to the ongoing human saga and forward progression of the human species. In fact the road ahead is beginning to look more like a runway. I appreciate your reading of this article and hope you will enjoy the discussion and thoughts it evokes. Perhaps this article is of interest to propel thought?

Artificial Intelligence and Decision Making Computer Software

Currently many industries are developing artifical intelligence software and decision matrix protocols to evaluate and determine the best choice of action for a given scenario. In the future probability and complexity will be no match for such tools. One will be able to ask a question and get a relevant and best possible answer within extremely short amount of times. Even NASA scientists are now developing such software, which will be able to evaluate options for mining materials for life support, colony building materials and refueling in lunar factories.

The most advanced of these artificial intelligent decision-making computer software systems can now rate and compare more than five different types of lunar or Martian Base station manufacturing systems and compare components of each for the best possible choices. In the future more and more criteria will be added to insure the best possible decision for the situation. For instance using the Moon as our platform to manufacture in Space to service needs of Manned Mars Exploration.

Humans will ask these artificially intelligent supercomputers how they came to a decision. The answer alone may not be enough. Some might say that people trust calculators and therefore they will trust the decisions of artificial intelligent computers and yet that may not be the case all the time.

For an artificial intelligent computer to really do a good job in decision-making it will have to put its human counterpart at ease and show them how IT came to the decision and break it down into pieces. Eventually the humans will come to trust the artificial intelligent computers, but until then humans will be demanding more answers in the form of more questions.

Humans will want to see the data sets and a deconstructed decision-making process in a format they can understand and this too will be a challenge for artificial intelligent computer software designers.

AI Programming for Decision Matrix Evaluation Theory; Case Study

When programming artificial intelligent systems to make decisions and or evaluate there are a number of theories that should be explored before choosing a specific path. Writing code is tedious and time consuming indeed and it is appropriate to do as much up front work as possible. First and foremost you need to decide on which model your AI system will take in its decision making process. If you intend to build a decision matrix system then you may wish to do a little philosophical discussion with yourself or your team. For instance think of ways in which mankind normally chooses things?

For instance in a beauty contest each woman would be given a numerical value on each event. Then after three to five events the woman with the highest score wins? In the

Winter Olympics in 2006 each judge had their own method of figuring things out and perhaps give consideration either objectively or subjectively to things such as technical work, creativity, uniqueness, performance and difficulty and come up with a score and thus use that to judge. All we see is a little card which says 9.8, 9.9 or a perfect "10" you see?

Now then on these two evaluation processes you can see how you might design your program to do these things. In the event of Winter Olympics Ice Skating with many judges you might mimic this in your artificial intelligence program by simply running several slightly different programs.

Humans will ask these artificially intelligent supercomputers how they came to a decision. The answer alone may not be enough. Some might say that people trust calculators and therefore they will trust the decisions of artificial intelligent computers and yet that may not be the case all the time.

For an artificial intelligent computer to really do a good job in decision-making it will have to put its human counterpart at ease and show them how IT came to the decision and break it down into pieces. Eventually the humans will come to trust the artificial intelligent computers, but until then humans will be demanding more answers in the form of more questions.

Humans will want to see the data sets and a deconstructed decision-making process in a format they can understand and this too will be a challenge for artificial intelligent computer software designers.

AI Programming for Decision Matrix Evaluation Theory; Case Study

When programming artificial intelligent systems to make decisions and or evaluate there are a number of theories that should be explored before choosing a specific path. Writing code is tedious and time consuming indeed and it is appropriate to do as much up front work as possible. First and foremost you need to decide on which model your AI system will take in its decision making process. If you intend to build a decision matrix system then you may wish to do a little philosophical discussion with yourself or your team. For instance think of ways in which mankind normally chooses things?

For instance in a beauty contest each woman would be given a numerical value on each event. Then after three to five events the woman with the highest score wins? In the Winter Olympics in 2006 each judge might have their own method of figuring things out and perhaps give consideration either objectively or subjectively to things such as technical work, creativity, uniqueness, performance and difficulty and come up with a score and thus use that to judge. All we see is a little card which says 9.8, 9.9 or a perfect "10" you see?

Now then on these two evaluation processes you can see how you might design your program to do these things. In the event of Winter Olympics Ice Skating with many judges you might mimic this in your artificial intelligence program by simply running several slightly different programs of numerical evaluations (each one similar to a judge) and then average the scores for a total score. This might work good for choosing one product, person or concept over another. On the beauty contest you might have many judges with similar ways of grading and slightly different subjectivity over various things within each event. This too can be duplication with programming for an artificial system quite easily.

Another humanly way we do things is to have contests where we pit two different teams against each other and the winner advances and the loser does not. Kind of like basketball playoffs or soccer championships. Or the NFL to determine at the end of the year who is the best. This form of evaluation can easily be programmed and such code is readily available. Using techniques of double or triple elimination you can better evaluate and remove much of the randomness of chance or luck and improve probability for coming up with not necessarily the absolute answer, but statistically speaking the best probable answer down to a point in 'which you can feel good that your AI computer system is fair, honest and in the end has chosen the best possible answer.

Now then when evaluating evaluation decision matrix artificial intelligent systems one must also realize that you are only limited by your creativity to pick the best system to evaluate. You might even write separate systems which uses all three of these systems or more and then average them together, thus getting closer to the unattainable best possible perfect choice. Why is this important? Well, if you expect humans to follow the orders of artificial intelligence systems then you should make sure than their answers that they come up with are truly 99.999999999% the best possible answer. Think on this in 2006.

Trucking Convoys of the Future and Artificial Intelligence

In the future vehicles including trucks, actually especially trucks will line up by size and run down the highway at higher rates of speed only feet from the bumpers of those in front of them. This will save lots of fuel due to the aerodynamic synergy gained and allow for more vehicles to travel with far less traffic congestion. Sounds like a plan!

But this is just a start because cashing in on the efficiencies in Coefficients of Drag in Convoys has lots of applications and may even change the current shape of our cars too. Indeed as these vehicles drive this close together there will be no room for driver error and thus the vehicles will talk to each other in a net-centric way.

The United States Military will have such convoys by 2012 and we will see the first Military Convoys within a few years and we are already seeing the first Self-Driving Turcks thanks to the DARP A Challenge Contests. Other strategies might include Tmck Trains and Multiple Trailers being power by one vehicle or one driver controlling an entire line of trucks which will mimic, his control input sequences.

What about using the air to move cargo such as Blimps or Dirigible Cargo Movers? What about the Flying Trucks of the Future? We were promised flying cars, what about flying trucks too? Don't laugh, because the same people who are considering this are also currently designing Net-Centric Systems to Guide Trucks.

Even NASA is thinking here as they consider ways to mine the moon, yes you guessed it: Lunar and Mars Mining Trucks. All this technology is on its way and it will not be long now. Of course one question remains with all this high-tech trucking hardware" Who will work on it, as currently there is a shortage of truck mechanics that is getting worse?

Well in the future there will be Robotic Diagnostics Systems and Artificial Intelligent AI Manuals to assist new technicians with all this complex and complicated computerized systems. The future cometh, so be ready.

UAVs to Plant Cactus Along the Mexican Border: The Thick Pointy Kind!

The amount of money budgeted to put up a border fence between the United States and Mexico is a staggering multi-billion-dollar project. Recently, our Online Think Tank considered some possible alternatives. And in doing so we left nothing off-limits, all ideas were discussed no matter how crazy; complete unlimited thought to solve this grave problem.

One idea was to put landmines along the border, which were nonlethal and they would pop up and put sleeping gas in the area putting all the border crossing people to sleep and then the discharged device would contact the satellite or radio in the location and alert authorities to go pick them up.

Another idea was to use UAVs to Plant Cactus along the Mexican Border: The Thick Pointy Kind! How would this work you ask? Well, the UAV would fly along in a grid pattern and drop seeds for cactus plants a few days before a storm was about to hit then we simply let nature take its course and the cactuses would grow tall and thick and make a permanent barrier to entry.

Over 500 people die each year crossing the deserts from Mexico into the United States and if the cactuses would prevent them from crossing they would have to turn back and they would not die of over heat exhaustion and lack of water. By planting cactuses we can save many lives.

UAV; Hunter II and RQIA Predator UAVs Additional Mods

Since the Predator has inverted "V" shaped stabilizers these stabilizers should contain wheel pants and wheels underneath to lessen weight and save costs in manufacturing, we need to bring down the costs of these units. Less mechanism will save weight and we can use that savings in weight for increased payload or more fuel to extend loitering time. I propose the rear Landing gear incorporated into this V-Tail assembly. Let's move Murphy out of these aircraft and keep it simple, cheap to build and efficient.

This is being proposed to reduce costs of future VAV squadrons in manufacturing and to save weight and fuel efficiency for longer missions and greater range to provide eyes in the sky and security to the battlespace and our nations and allied borders. Redesigning UAV choices in your battlespace UAV siumulations and computer games will be necessary to keeping pace with the real world war planners as the technology hyperspaces the world of virtual reality.

Many of the current UAV models are being looked at for improvement in efficiency for added range, additional payload and stealth. Are you designs viable, are they better than actual? Are you learning from aerospace engineers or are you still teaching them lessons in what works?

UAV Materials and Thoughts on New Technologies and Keeping Up With Our Opponents

Possible UAV matenals are infinite: Foam, Composite, Balsa Wood, Plastic, Synthetic Balloon Material, Aluminum, Titanium, Spider Web Organic Material, etc. I propose some late breaking technology and newer materials, ceramic coatings and or UAVs built from photorefractive composites? Materials such as this:

http://www.tech-db.ru/istc/db/pra.nsf/pran/1273

Why? Weight, stealth, parasite drag, induced drag, boundary layers, and performance. NASA is looking into this as well for other uses;

http://www. aist-nara. ac. jp/~orieken!

Then there are some really awesome practitioners, which have it all figured out, UAV manufacturing companies have come alive in the last decade; even Plastics are used in UAVs especially the smaller ones. The larger UAV are made out of just about anything you can imagine. We are not the only ones learning about what to make these out of and we are not the only country capable of making them, many other countries arc trying new things also. So it is important to be the best at it and have ways to shoot down enemy UAVs.

Recently there was a major news story in the media about the FBI working on finding espionage theft of secret research. One spokesmen, head of the group in Mountain View, CA, said next to International Terrorism it is the FBI's number 2 priority as the loss of important research is leaving the country way too fast; citing that our trading partners and allies were also spying on us; Chinese, Israel, Japan, Pakistan, Iran. And you only have to read the news occasionally to know this is a real issue. Top Secret means about 6 months until it is all over the Internet.

Classified means 3 months before some reporter gets a hold of it and it is for this reason that UAV technologies are so dangerous and why we must keep up the innovations in this area to stay ahead of our competition.

As technology progresses, your enemy will have the same tools and technologies you do, by buying it from an ally, spy or secretly stealing it from a University Research Team. So when you invent something as weapon for offense or defense of your people, you have to know how to defeat it too. As it will be used against you in a court of law (war).

Most all foreign countries have UAV programs and have established research and development teams and put forth spies on the subject as well as pretend collaborators. We need to pay attention for the bettennent of NATO Countries and UN participants. But what about hostile or potentially hostile nations, they have scientists too.

Unmanned Flight is now capable in nearly any current aircraft with the exception of the skill necessary to fly and take-off in a Ryan Monoplane or those requiring the balance of a pilot such as a hang glider or ultra light like the crash and burn motorcycle team brave enough to give it a test at the DARPA Grand Challenge, hats go off to that team for a noble and worthy attempt.

If you think for one second that North Korea does not have UAVs of some type to augment their arsenal of Ballistic capable nuclear missiles think again. They trade with China and Japan and both have established programs, The Trade with South Korea and we have UAVs in Country and North Korea has spies there too.

Even Saddam had a UAV prototype Hying bomb program, some would say was in it's infancy, I say bull all they needed was a motor attached, you can buy that at an ultra-light store or online catalog, no one can deny that, google for yourself if you find folly with my observation. A device such as that prototype UAV with a chemical compound or pathogen, virus or disease in it is not very funny if dispersed into a large city. These technologies are available and are or have been in all the arsenals of the Axis of Evil Countries.

http://cns.miis.edu/pubs/week/030408.htm

I am not the only person worried of this. UAVs that we build need to be light-weight, good payload, stealthy and agile. But the enemy due to cost may decide to build a huge number of cheap units and bet on the numbers rather than survivability, so can we defeat a swann of these?

Very similar scenario, which scared all American's during the cold war, shooting down multiple ICBM warheads which scatter and attack pre-assigned cities. Some UAV enemy strategies include a different approach to the notion of single mission non-recovery theory as many academics have eluded to in the reports online.

I would have to agree that money to buy the units is a big factor as our Congress appropriated much monies to the predator program for DHS and Military, smart move. Coast Guard, Boarder Patrol, etc., but if a UAV does not do very much in the way of surveillance or ordinance delivery due to payloads in smaller non-predator type UAVs then a smart bomb maybe a better way to go once air defenses have been taken out of the equation, which is why we are well served to have both technologies available to us.

Of course it also depends how many targets, time frame and economics of scale when it comes to the logistical costs of movements of people, fuel, food, weapons and power.

Every mission should have a cost benefit and a goal oriented solution, that of course being the name of the game, to win it. UAVs provide options, lower costs over all and smart planning and curtail loss of life on both sides. Single mission UAVs, small versions are appropriate in many regards. Predators are good in that they can be used forever unless we start crashing them.

These smaller UAVs, like SmartBombs are especially important during regime changes when your goal is to provoke change in leadership not in destroying vast amounts of individual human life, no matter what amount of value is placed on it by the culture opposing your political will, but taking out those who oppose the will of the free World and stability of the Human Race.

Nevertheless, war is hell, so you must win at all costs, which goes without saying, losing sucks and defeat or retreat cannot be an option for our team. Retreat should only be used as a tactic to serve your future will. Let the enemy re-group and congregate and attack again getting most bang for your buck.

UAVs are here to stay and will require proper funding, such Rand D will come back ten fold to mankind in potential commercial uses for moving freight within and out side our own atmosphere, for doing jobs in agriculture, short and small delivery and of course the future of air travel pilot less commercial aircraft much the same as the NYC subways and people movers across the country and throughout the world.

The costs of UAVs are important and the materials provide the efficiencies necessary to make them light, fast, manoeuverable and strong. By watching the costs and picking the right materials, we can always maintain the lead in UAV research and Development, Deployment and acquiring of target to stay in front of the pack in the never ending Human Saga, of Good VS Evil.

You know the Sound and Fury stuff, which has been going on since all of the recorded history we know about. We sure are funny, us humans? Wonder if we will ever figure it out?

Battery Signature Sensors to Detect Enemy UAVs

We must develop a new type of radar sensor one which can see an unmanned aerial vehicle even if it is made of lightweight material with little if any radar signature or it is of a superior shape, which is hard to see. In the future UAVs both ours and our enemies will indeed run on the latest high-tech futuristic batteries being charged by fuel cells.

If the new morphing techniques eliminate much of the drag and the wake turbulence signature and if the aircraft are silent and if the aircraft give off little or no heat; then how can you see them? Well, how about the frequency difference between batteries and electromagnetic energy in statie air and are bient air. I propose we start now ahead of this game and design and build such a detection device to pick up battery energy and record those anomalies as disruptions for detection of enemy UAVs.

Further since this strategy will be used in the future we must figure out new materials to hide this energy and ways re-direct the electric signature of batteries back into a close loop system which indeed prevent any detectable anomaly. How much money should be allotted to this? Well if you consider the amount of unmanned aerial vehicle expenditures and the cost to replace them if an enemy shoots them all down and how that would render much of our flying robotic war strategy in the modern net-centric battlespace; then I would say a bundle. Think on this in 2006.

Override Evasion Software for Telelmatic UAVs

Our Unmanned Aerial Vehicles have proven themselves in the battles pace to be some of our most important assets. These UAVs have also been used fighting fires, guarding our borders and helping in disasters. Many of these UAVs are controlled by line of sight communication command and control systems, while others can be controlled remotely via satellites. When these UAVs are controlled via satellite there is a one second delay in commands from the desktop pilot who is basically operating from a PC with a joystick and some instruments, not a whole lot different than Microsoft Simulator Program you buy in the store. This system works well when you are merely flying around looking at statu and sending back the video feed to command and control.

There comes a problem when you need instantaneous manoeuvering and are also dealing with the reality of situational awareness from a UAV and also with the time delay in directions from the virtual pilot in augmented reality at command and control. However many things such as evasion could be preprogrammed for dodging SAMs (surface to air missiles) shot from an enemy.

If you have to wait for the communication delays it could be too late for your drone UAV. Once the UAV takes the drastic measures to evade the SAM, it would then seek normal flight on the former heading or a heading of exactly 180 degrees from where it started. Thus it has evaded, recorded the location from where the missile was fired and retreated. Now you can assign the launch location of the SAM as a legitimate target.

A UAV has an advantage over a fighter aircraft with a pilot, as it can turn with more G's as long as stay with in its envelope. Indeed there would be the same control limits for flight departure issues as in the newest of fighters when you travel outside the envelope, which would be massively expanded with new materials, lack of biological needs of a pilot and directional thrust tricks of the trade and intake air opening changes in-night all computerized.

As a pilot myself "single engine land," I do not want to ditch the pilots just yet for the silicon chip versions. Especially as I look at the cost of some of these high tech advanced UAVs, after all that is an expensive piece of hardware, but we are seeing more and more evidence of Big Blue beating the best chess players of the air. In the end our decision must be for the mission, not our debate over organic VS autonomous or robotic, I guess I would say, I just want to WIN, that is all; using the whole track is that was the first thing they told us in racing school, it helped keep me alive. We need to do whatever it takes, for however long it takes to accomplish the mission. Whatever that might be. It is only about winning. But we cannot send a UAV into an area laden with the enemy that has shoulder fired or batteries of surface to air missiles unless they robotic counterparts have master evasion software programs, which immediately over ride the command and control and autonomously address the threat. Think on this.

Launching 400 UAVs from a Transport Plane

How to launch hundreds of UAV s for an autonomous mission from a transport plane. As we watched the MOAB parachute bomb drop out of a C-130 onto the desert and above the tunnels below into Afghanistan. It left the world in awe. Now then this parachute concept has another idea. Launching UAVs, hundreds of them in swarms of 25 to 50, to overwhelm the opponent.

Here is how it is done, the little cute UAVs are put into a bread rake type configuration but like a box made of plastic or composite. It is thrown out the back of the aircraft, okay see ya. Then the parachute opens. The UAVs are launched by relative wind as they dive down after release.

Large propellers to start the motors since the motors would have high compression. Or the propellers would spin and break the small cellophane wall separating the chemicals in a little bag allowing them to combine and become a battery.

As the box slows down and the parachute deploys air pressure from under the box would cause the bottom to fall out since it would be on a spring and simply pop off and fall to Earth or it could hang there in an open vertical position until the launching device hit the ground and the door hitting first would trigger and explosion destroying any un-launched aircraft and the box it self, if made of composite it would of course burn cyanide gas so no one would attempt to go near it until it was finally all burned up. As each floor released its aircraft then the next floor would spring back since all the weight of the UAV were gone and the relative air pressure from the slowly dropping parachute started the next set of UAVs on that floor.

The falling UAVs would have some stability and of course dihedral and would simply start flying and the satellite would ping them to keep them flying where ever they were to go. Once in real close; each UAV would go to its exact target, usually five to six per target to be sure, low cost allows for this.

Once the aircraft were dropped out the bottom their higher rate of speed and lower drag than the parachute would easily clear them and the lift from the wing would allow them lateral separation. A small tooth pick could have the horizontal stabilizer in the up position as a temporary trim tab which would come off as the aircraft increased its speed, hut stay on long enough to clear the chute. This set up could be used in a C-130, C-5, C-141, C-17 with such ease it would not even be funny.

You could even fly these UAVs in all directions and put flairs on them so they would have a big heat signature or pop out a piece of tin foil or drag a large metallic piece of exmpled aluminum to attract a radar and lock for anti-aircraft or SAM missiles and thus draw fire while AWACs watched pin-point targets and launched against all known radar sites, All because the enemy was fooled by model aircraft.

There are hundreds of types of scenarios and uses for these devices. The cool thing is they do not even have to be viable, work or be operational. It simply sends your opponent in so many misdirectional scenarios it overwhelms them and makes them hesitate to act, thus not commit and gives you the superior edge to make your opponent question themselves.

By flying UAVs with quarter mile spacing launched separately and turning them on in sequence you could mimic a flight speed of an F-18 and they would assume the incoming is a stealth which is remotely showing up occasionally or an F-18 coming in fast. Thus such a threat looks real and they have to turn on their systems to fire upon it. But it does not exist and all they will get after firing the SAM is a model airplane and have given away their position or possibly not even get the UAV, the one in the lead. Then you kill the SAM sight and turn the UAVs in another direction and keep going, they will never figure out what you are doing. Each time they simply at maximum get the lead UAV, which is relatively cheap considering you scored a SAM sight and will soon have air superiority for free basically.

By launching UAVs in all directions with different signatures you could mimic an all out attack from the wrong location, while your enemy sends resources to fight the diversion you are attacking key targets within other territories. A few times of this and they will stop chasing ghosts and then you arm the little UAVs and use them. Or use a stealth with the similar mimicking signature and they think it is simply a dud crying wolf.

You have to value the UAV scenarios. A weapon to prevent war, by eliminating threats which kill people on your team, making it easy to go in to get your exact target to serve your political will with no worries of reciprocal responses which will cost lives on your side. This is most perfect for regime change.

No collateral damage and you do not even need a bunch of military lawyers deciding what a proper target is against an enemy who most likely would cut off the balls of one of your captured infantry and shove them in their mouth cut off the head and parade it around town. We are so polite in warfare yet our opponents so barbaric. War is hell and you must bring hell to you enemy.

If your real enemy is the regime leaders, you must eliminate defenses and go get them ASAP, that is the best for all concerned and in that sense if war can ever be humane, as we kill members of our own species and continue this notion of war, then this must be the way it is done.

Some day there will not be wars, although a man who would not be willing to fight for what they believe in is not a man, and therefore we must evolve into something else or all believe in the same thing.

That same thing could be a religion if you will, a sense of Earth pride, World Nationalism provided we arc all of one nation, or admit to ourselves are all together and we are all of planet Earth. Or we need to unite the world as one and possibly all have a common enemy such as "Evil" "mediocrity" etc. Asteroids, whatever, and something to name so we can unite.

But until then, in a sense we are still a warring species, we ought to find the best way to serve our will with the least amount of future conflict as war is an escalation of political will, which has advanced past the level of reason by one or more of the disagreeing parties.

Too philosophical? May be, perhaps, but you must admit the UAV Swarm idea is part of our future.

BMPs for Killing Hostile UAVs

We need to set up Best Management Practices for shooting down enemy unmanned aerial vehicles. There are many reasons for this directive for instance; we must make sure what we are shooting is really an enemy UAV and not one of our own; that it is not a friendly force craft; that it is not a civilian aircraft which happened into our net-centric security grid or kill box.

Additionally an enemy UAV will generally have a mission, whether it is a single mission as a flying bomb or a surveillance mission and will return to base. If it is surveillance unmanned aerial vehicles then by the time you see it, it may have already recorded your assets and their locations and killing it serves no purpose as the cat it now out of the bag. However if we track and follow it via satellite, radar or other flying vehicle, we can learn a lot. Such as where did it come from and if you kill it straight away, then you will never know where it learn from. If you follow it, you now have a very valuable target of your enemy's command and control. If you shoot it down with a missile, it will sense the missile coming at it and attempt to evade while simultaneously registering the launch point of the surface to air missile and earn transmit that information prior to being hit. However if you do decide to kill a territory crossing or border violating UAV it is best to kill it from the air rather than give away anti aircraft battery points on the ground which are fixed and will become a future target for your enemy.

Where as if you shoot it down from the air via Airborne High Energy Laser then the UAV is killed at the speed of light, cannot know where it came from, even if it figures it out, it cannot transmit while under that level of high energy as the signal will be broken. Additionally if it is hit from above it may not have visual acuity or situational awareness from above. These are just a few of the many things we must be thinking of to come up with strategic best management practices for killing enemy UAVs. We need to be thinking here, as soon our enemy's will be considering sending in robotic weapons to kill us.

Drawing Hand Held Surface to Air Missile Fire at Night Using UAVs

One of the easiest ways to draw shoulder launched missiles at night is to fly UAVs very close and use the simulated sound of an Apache Attach Helicopter, Howling of a jet fighter or a few UAVs flying together the combined sound of a four engine transport. At night you could have a few UAVs with strobe lights or a tint of green glow simulating reflections off the canopy of an attack helicopter along with sound used by a whistler on the UAV, or even a whistler, which mimicked a high frequency sound which caused their equipment to whistler.

Devices such as these can be bought at Wal-mart for five dollars, the faster the UA V travels the more sound or high frequency sound is made. We also use these on cars in deer country, but certain ones screw with your radio reception you know? Every time a shoulder missile is launched they have one less. Chances are it will not even hit the target anyway, they will launch it into the sky and nothing will happen, may not even come close, they will probably launch it too far in front of the UAV assuming a rate of speed for an aircraft which is not even there.

A UAV could also go into an area near a border crossing using electric battery power or glide in after turning off the motor and crash 300 feet from the enemy troops. Have a small glow and cigarette smell and a small set of voices talking about getting laid in English and the newest corvette model the enemy would sneak up on the crashed model plane and give away their positions and could be seen by night vision goggles.

We can even see small arm fire from satellites now, if they sent of a mortar round, we are all over it, never know what hit them or see where it came from. You certainly would have less people fighting you if you had stories like that floating around that is if anyone lived to tell anyone else what happened that night?

How Soon Will UAVs Make Fighter Pilots Obsolete?

Unmanned Aerial Vehicles are rapidly making human fighter pilots obsolete. Flight be better to use a UAV and to that have it down by a 16-year old video game player, which will in turn be used to program the next generation of Artificial Intelligent robotic tactical UAVs. How can this be happening so fast? Well, it is not really happening very fast, as they have had drones for decades and missiles for at least six decades. Artificial Intelligence is making the difference.

Old mainframes with tape drives did not learn like in Artificial Intelligence of today, but you must remember, you can program a tic-tac-toe game into a computer and it will never lose, only draw. It will never lose. MIT proved that, but if you think on it; you will know this simply be reasoning as tic-tac-toe is a simple game with simple miles. This is basic Tinker Toy Logic, it is all one's and zero's, there is an X in cell or grid 1, "0" in cells 4 and 5 the rest are empty. Then: are only 6 possible answers. If the computer is the "X's" it chooses grid space 6, to block. You chose you "0" in box or grid space 3, it blocks space seven draw.

If it is playing a human and the human messes up one time in any game the computer will win that game. The computer does not get tired and will play until you unplug it. You will eventually mess up, you are human and to be human is to error. If you as a fighter pilot choose a different game, it has most likely encountered or been programmed it. If you are totally creative you may choose a manoeuvre, strategy or game it does not recognize or has not been programmed for and you might win? But what if it is relaying the data to other units in the battles pace and over all system, which the computer UAV now knows that; did not work and will disengage if encountered until it has been programmed for such as manoeuvre? Whereas if you lose, it wins, you are dead and it now knows it can beat you if you do that.

I believe we can design a computer better than the average human and since there are so few innovators in any walk of life, granted fighter pilots, more than other sectors; you may lose a few dogfights, but will still lose the war to the UAVs with artificial intelligence. Eventually the human cannot win, and you may wish to think bragging about being 100% human now. There ain't a whole lot that is very special about this carbon based biped. Consider these thoughts when designing UAVs with artificial intelligence.

Piloted Aircraft or Computerized Artificial Intelligent UAVs

Currently our artificial intelligence research is not quite as good as a human organic brain however it win not be long before computers can beat a human in a dog fight. 'There are many limitations to an organic human to a UAV with special electronics, which can withstand 18 G's. Pilots black out at 8 to 10 G's thus giving up an advantage to the "aggressor" computerized version. However a pilot thinks and can change the game and miles to win, whereas a computer program is based on a complex set of rules.

Indeed a computer has disadvantages as it cannot think and adapt, yet as we design them to learn or program themselves and share that information with the entire whole of all the other computers mining all the other units in the robotic net-centric battlespace, everything will change forever. I propose we must get to that point if we expect to send computers and robots to war to serve our political will. With such a system developed and battlebots, UAVs and computers learning and programmed themselves; you will need one hell of a pilot to overcome that consistently. I would bet on the computer or I would act on me. But I would not necessarily put my money on any old human fighter pilot, for most will die in that scenario and it is coming in the future, we should not kid ourselves. That statement is not coming from science fiction authors; in fact that is coming from deductive reasoning and observing humans doing things in all aspects of their life experiences over and over again, often making the same mistake (doomed to repeat).

Let's face it even a racket ball master tournament winner knows it takes 25,000 strokes to commit an action to muscle memory. Fighter Pilots just do not have that kind of time and you know we do not teach, train or school humans to think anymore, we train them to react a certain way to a certain problem. Only those who can think will win. I know so few, how about you? Luckily presently most war planners and robotic research scientists are currently pro-human pilot or should I say "no pilot left behind:" but in the end that will only mean all humans left behind if we are not honest with the obvious future.

We will develop computers, which cannot be beaten by the current organic human brains. Either we upgrade the human brain thru DNA manipulation and computer interface assist or humans will lose to those who control the robots and thus the battle will be one before it is fought. I propose that be the side that is doing what it right and for the right reasons. I propose we spend massive amounts on robotic research to insure that is our team.

If you doubt the potential of this possible future, think for a second, as we already have U AVs, which down aircraft they are called SAMs with a "single mission" in mind to kill a human piloted aircraft. And we have missiles, which shoot down other missiles, which is kind of a dummy Computer VS. Computer war; or Robot VS Robot isn't it? No one can claim that no human has ever been shot down by a SAM able to handle 18 G's. Even when the pilot wins the enemy could simply change its strategy and what do you do when they shoot three or (2) sets of three at your human pilot, as they watch their airspeed and manoeuverability bleed off? Eject? why? Because you are out of cards, airspeed, visual overload, lack of situational awareness and still have two-more coming at you and if they fail another set of three, until you die or piss. Robots and computers arc already beating human fighter pilots, if you really think about it from a more abstract point. Think on this.

Improvements in Loitering Single Mission UAVs

We are seeing some new trends in Unmanned Aerial Vehicles or UAVs, in fact we arc seeing hybrids of sorts. Smart Bombs and Missiles which fly around all day and then select a target. Sometimes wings which pop-put then fly to the target or some other models well the wings just fall off and the missile or bomb falls to shoots to the target.

Originally these technologies were secretive, but now they are in the open. And if nothing more it puts the fear of Allah into our enemy indeed. As the meeting appears to be pre-arranged if they arc looking to die in battle, well the new battles pace is owned, bought and paid for compliments of the US Taxpayer and Uncle Sam's big stick. One of these technology hybrids, which I do not think the project is classified although parts of it could be is the missile which shoots into the battles pace at high speed waits around all day, then selects and confirms a target and then takes out said target: Hardly a negotiating process, game over for the enemy, out of quarters.

If you would like to learn more then go to the DARPA website and read the AFRL Air Force Research Laboratory Annual report, which indeed makes mention of this technology. You will also find reference to it in Aviation Leak and Spy Technology they had complete diagrams on the concept before anything was ever started and subsequent follow-ups recently.

Indeed also realize that with the new steerable mortar rounds and large shells using NLOS directional controls can do nearly the same thing. The biggest issues is in the future with China taking out Satellites and such in case of a non-appeasement deal with their reunification of Taiwan. We know that their University level kids are good at math and are writing almost as many scientific papers as we are currently. Even such we must realize that as they educate and if the leadership uses us as an enemy "evil" figure to build up their team, then we will continue to have their spies stealing our stuff here and then perfecting it there. They are already working on Seismic Inducing Machines, Weather Modification, Mind Control and Biological weapons (even testing it on their own people in Eastern and South Eastern Provinces) that is to say the recent Bird Flu Vaccine. What I am saying is we must continually innovate and understand that the future is moving faster than ever before and these UAV technologies are a major component in the net-centric battles pace of the future and our nation's security and future longevity as the leader of the free world depend on them. Think on this.

Artificial Intelligence Debate for UAVs Vs Manned Aircraft in the Battlespace

Mankind is fascinating with making artificial intelligence, which can compete with 150 million years of humankind and their organic brains. Many kids growing up are being introduced to robotic systems and many colleges and universities are hot on the trail at advancing our knowledge in what we call artificial intelligence. But we have been designing computers to compete with mankind for decades. A few books ago, I was reading; "'A Shortcut through Time; The Path to the Quantum Computer" by George Johnson, he made a note of that Tinker Toy Tic Tac Toe Machine, Geniac Electric Brain construction kit, 'furing Computer, Blue Mountain, etc.. I recommend this book to anyone who is studying these concepts of Man VS Computer.

Some get carried away with the. Concept of Human VS. Machine and the programming and thought processes, but it strikes at the core of the Pilot VS. UAV s debate indeed. Such basic background does enter into the picture with UAV and fighter aircraft survivability in combat; Man VS. Machine. I guess if you are interested in learning more of the thinking and theory behind these ideas a good first stop might be Ray Kurzweil's AI website:

http://www.kurzweilai.net/index.html?f1ash =2

For now the artificial intelligence Debate for UAVs VS. Piloted Aircraft in the Battlespace rages on and indeed the argument is taken to greater heights and a whole new level, a deadly one as it is a "winner take all" game. Can the humans really beat computers, which teach themselves and can think as fast or faster than their human counterpatis? Think on this, as you will hardly be alone in those thoughts.

Verbal Commands to Fly UAVs

Autonomous Artificial Intelligent Unmanned Aerial V chicles is not a new concept, after all Sci Fi writers have been discussing it for years. We are truly getting closer to such technologies and it may become a reality sooner than we think. The next step for unmanned vehicles whether they be on the ground, air, sea or a combination of all three, will soon work on verbal commands.

A military commander will simply say to the Unmanned Aircraft to go fly over sector III and VI and alert us if there are any red force still alive: oh and watch out for SAMs (surface-to-air missiles). The UAV will then fly off, choose its best optimum speed based on the intensity of the command voice, fly to the sectors in the order commanded, turn on anti -missile avoidance system on level 5 (highest evasion program) and then send in a video feed narrated as it flies. It will then come back and land and wait for another command while it alerts other robotics on the ground to refuel it and then it will hibernate, just like your laptop does when it is on batteries? Sound too far out? Well if you think five years is too far out, then you are right But I say it is right around the corner for DARP A and military service or Department of Homeland Security.

Imagine robots, which you simply talk to them in your own language; "go put out that fire," or better yet "clean the pool and wash the RV while I am gone, oh and alert me if the check comes in the mail Thanks!"

Generally such technology is first seen in military or space application and then within a few more years it can find its way into commercial purposes. Expect this to be available for you at home in 6-8 years or less through one of the leading robot makers such as iRobot, US Robotics or a Japanese manufacturer of robots. Some say much sooner? Think on this.

UAVs to Penetrate Massive Enemy Defense Systems

In the event of an enemy with missile defense systems, border security and armed guards a UAV maybe the only choice. A UAV with real time video could be remotely controlled much like a model aircraft and fly into the target area. In the event the target was a small group of enemy leaders or the command and control center this tactic could work if you could get within 10-20 miles. No matter what modern day defenses the enemy has you can fly right past them unencumbered directly to the target.

A single mission UAV in the form of a large model aircraft could do the attack on the enemy relatively easy. Let us look at some of the inexpensive units available, which you can build in country. This might be the perfect tactic for our CIA, to take out the enemy commanders and generals. Model Airplane hobby folks have long known of the servos you can buy which allow a model aircraft to make a practice bomb run.

http://www.mh.ttu.ee/risto/rc/logo20;build/page09/page09.htm

They have contests to see who can drop a small bad of flour closest to a red "X" using a remote control command and a servo which when activated releases the bad of flour. Read some of the rules that are used in conjunction with some of the contests:

http://www.sirs-rc.com/rules .html

See this page and look at the Dehavilland Hornet, you can order it with Bomb Drop Servos already installed? Perfect for CIA use and covert actions.

http://www.carstens-publications.com/plans...=&returnpage= 10

Replace flour with hand grenades and we have a very good single mission UAV killing machine. Then make the wing spar out of C-4 drop. The CIA can build the airplane without concern nearly every country has such hobbyists. Today you can by model hobby video feed for your large model, which allows you to see where you are flying too. Feel free to google this and you will see the many options readily available to the online buyer.

The operator can operate from 20 miles away from, high vantage point. He can operate across borders, from the top of a bridge support or large building. Able to penetrate defense batteries, go thru areas of high security, border crossings and ground protection. The UAV model which has been bought and built locally outfitted with such basic infantry weaponry can their fly low level to take out the bad guys. An electric UAV cannot be shot down with a small shoulder fired missile if it is made an electric motor. No air defenses can hit it and when the US Army tired to shoot one down they were unable, so as long as the unit flies fast and low, chances are nearly 100% that it can penetrates tens of millions of dollars worth of defensive measures.

If you are still concerned they will shoot it down, although I guarantee you that will never happen, you can disguise it as a big bird? The leadership of Iran or North Korea spending millions and millions to protect their top commanders would have no chance as the CIA flies right in with a model airplane and drops the grenades and then flies like a Kamikaze into the human military leaders who have declared war against us.

Hypothetical of course since they have not declared war on us yet. As a tactic to take out enemy command and control or Military leaders we should be considering model aircraft attacks. Many model airplanes could be sent simultaneously to insure the targets are eliminated. No longer will we have to worry about a rogue dictator who due to his own paranoia has spent millions in security and put many defense barriers between himself and the human rights needs of the Free World. Just think all that can be achieved without a can-ier fleet, anny, trillions in logistical supply chain or the risk of hundreds of thousands of troops.

Defense System for Protecting Oil Refinery Assets Against Enemy UAVs

During the cold war we had a some very good ánti-aircraft and land based mobile missile defense systems. Could we take one of these systems and scale it down, miniaturize it and use it to defend and protect our oil refineries, infrastructure and national security interests? Could we take let's say a smaller and lighter version of the "Lance" mobile missile systems of the cold war with a similar theory and place it on a Sandia "Sarge" type tiny mobile autonomous unit. Then employ these robotic security systems along defendable perimeter locations?

We could put them on the border when we attack Canada and take some property off their hands for aiding and abedding International Terrorists, so if they tried to fly one of those little Israeli UAVs they are buying over our border we would dust it immediately. Just kidding, but we need to be thinking defense and offence here to have a proper discussion on anti-attack defense systems. Obviously we are not going to war with Canada, but we do have our enemies in the Middle East harboring International Terrorists and some State Sponsored Insurgents attacking our troops in Iraq? Could we use such a system like this there to prevent intrusions over the borders? Perhaps we could, but how you ask?

Well lets first look at the issues with guarding oil assets as the International Terrorists wish to take down our economy using oil as a weapon knowing we need the oil to run our civilization. If we pay humans to Carry weapons to patrol a perimeter of let's say an oil refinery then will they be able to take out a single mission UAV which will self destruct and explode on impact and even if they did hit it, which is highly unlikely, could they take out a swam of them? The answer is no, you have just lost you oil refinery asset.

Now then let us re-think a man-portable stinger missile type system, when you may have to worry about a swam of these little UAVs, each with 5-10 Ibs of plastic explosives or even a smaller payload per explosion of two-hand grenades, you see the problem. The International Terrorists may not be able to take out your entire refinery, but they might get lucky and start an uncontrollable fire.

Remember those Refinery fires outside of London, early reports, which were later denied said that an aircraft new over prior to the explosions? Well did they throw something out; if so what. Was that aircraft manned or was it a small UAV; if so could it have been shot down with an intercepting UAV devise or a man-portable unit; perhaps? But only if the security force was alerted, actually saw it and focus, identify and fire in time.

Could a man sit and wait to fire it? Do you want to put a unit such as this into the hands of a civilian $10 per hour security guard? Not me? That type of weapon in the hands of the wrong person who knew and was trained how to use it could be used to take out a commercial airliner. Not funny.

Yet if the International Terrorists continue to attack non -military soft targets for PR and oil or natural gas assets we have serious issues as we must defend the flows of our civilization right? So how about an Aerostat or UAV which is tethered on a track with a system on it to detect such an incoming threat which would interact with a robotic perimeter defense system then you could potentially defeat anything which comes close and thus defend such an asset? Think on this.

UAVs and the Future Enhancements of Tele-Robotics

Today we have already available UAVs, which will soon have the capacity of operating together in swarms, controlled from another nearby aircraft. We have UAVs, which can be flown by a pilot sitting at a desk more than 1000 miles away. We have trucks, which have virtual dashboards, which send back complete data to dispatchers and a similar version for aircraft, which allows one to fly the other.

If one UAV being flown by a human being sitting at a desk half way around the world can control a swam of UAVs in a given location and those UAVs can give such information from a disassociated position of total awareness to those on the ground then we already have the capabilities of doing this from a more complex modelling standpoint.

If we can send this information directly into a human mounted optical device, with complete GPS-GIS data then we are getting closer, when we can have 360 degree sight, along with infrared, heat signature, chemical composure, frequency variation and molecular makeup and that device interfaces with the brain and human function, thrusting the efficiencies of motion and control into new realms, what can be done effortlessly would have been though of as God-Like only years the prior. We need to design a completely tele-robotic system, which works at the speed of thought and is connected to the enhanced human brain for complete 5D total situational awareness using all the current technologies available.

The future of human evolution will include enhancements of our Mother Nature Baseline organic carbon based bipod units. Think about it.

UAV Decoy Strategies, Theories and the Modern Art of War

Well having studying the need for decreasing America's dependence on Foreign Oil and the advances of the automotive industry such as Fed Ex and OPS along with Eaton and GM. Also studying the efforts of Sunlite Bus in Palm Desert and the recent information on ceramic coatings and problems in Urban Heat, Ozone Levels, Global Warming Issues from NASA and GeoSat efforts and various weather updates and information gathering data efforts to predict thunder storms, Hurricanes, Fires and Tornados we have learned quite a bit.

Now then as we have studied the problems associated with fuel cells in the heat transfer process and the need to minimize heat escaping on 100's of thousands of vehicles on America's highways and in urban metro areas causing urban heat and the possible leakage of hydrogen tanks could cause problems in ozone and global warning as the number of vehicles across the country increase over the next four decades. But this all being me adds to the dilema of a "Hydrogen Economy" (recommended reading list). It is also the case that in most of mankinds dilemas we find the greatest opportunities. Such is the definition of Chaos as we see so often throughout or species most recent 10,000 years of recorded history.

The fact that hydrogen cells put out 1200 degree heat and certain fuel cell units using certain compounds give off more in this process means that their heat signature is greater than other types of aircraft. Which is a problem if one is powered by hydrogen cell because it is very easy to hit with a higher footprint if a surface to air heat seeking missile is used right? Yes this is obviously the enough.

Now then If small UAVs are created and we are talking about making 500 for such an effort and they can be built with tin foil and alluminum foil krinkled in their wings and have a high heal coming from their power plant then they are great targets for surface to air missiles. If the enemy thinks or even knows that UAVs are taking pictures of the ground then they will shoot at them. We know from trying to shoot down UAVs with small caliber machine guns or ritles that it is nearly impossible.

So then to down one of these things they need a missile, which will be able to hit them. However if the UAVs are cheap to make and we know they are if you study model aircraft any. Then you can make these with a fuel cell motor in mass for about $500.00 each. You could literally cause your enemy to run out of SAMs trying to down 500 UAVs and our cost would be little. $250K to guarantee that no SAMs were left. They could fly around all day and draw fire. Using Hydrogen they could stay aloft longer too.

The cost of losing a helicopter of fighter/attack aircraft is very high and the loss of life is still a larger factor in determining a wars success. We like to win after all we are Americans. So then remembering that the cost to train a single pilot in the military is $250K so then simply saving one pilot means we save 250K to retrain his replacement and save the possibly $15 million for the most inexpensive fighter. So we should be building UAVs on a huge scale, some for decoys too.

These units should have fuel cells which that technology is good for America for lawn mowers, ATVs, chain saws, pressure washers and lawn tractors. Thus we can assist in changing the oil economy slowly and fund the research through the military against those who oppose us for better means and save pilots and money to our military in the short Tenn. and long ton. There arc hundreds of web sites with this group of hobbyists:

http://wvvw.uoguelph.ca/"~antoon!websites/air.htm

and there are many new fuel cell devices which run small things.

http://www.japantoday.com/e/?content =news&cat=4&id==261833

You see you can drive your enemy nuts and if you have 500 UAVs there is safety in numbers and you can mimic the amount of heat signature of other aircraft by the type of fuel burned and the lack of ceramic coatings to shield the heat. You pick the temperature you want it to put out between 1200-2000 degrees and they can easily build you 500? After all, you are only taking the amount of energy need to keep aloft a small UAV with a 15 foot wingspan and some gadgetry. Also remember in WWII when we tried to figure out the German Radio frequencies they used so we could bomb them with out detection by scrambling that frequency?

Well we can put dummy devices in the UAVs set to dummy frequencies and then they will capture the ones which run out of gas and assume those are the RF photo transferring frequencies and then they will try to scramble the frequency which we are not using thus giving away their locations and we smart bomb them. Dumb idea huh? No perfect decoy game of hide and seek.

Also there are devices you can put on vehicles, which make sound like a whistle that hurt or are unpleasing to the human ear. Fly the UAV around and the piercing sound will affect them and make them irritated and then they will really want to blast these UAVs out of the sky at all costs. You know like when you have a few flays in the house after the 4th of July BBQ, you spend a considerable amount of human energy to kill a little fly which is spending 1:500,000 the energy you are. Talk about a waste of energy.

Of course this is the same theory, the enemy uses it's valuable resources to hit the little stupid UAV, and having done so makes them less able to hit your important aircraft. Including the non Decoy UAVs which are gathering your information.

If you fly these units at night they will have no idea what the heck it is, the radar shows high heat, large object. The opposite of Stealth. The UAV says "HELLO, I'M HERE, WATCHA GONNA DO NOW, HELLO!!!!"

There are older radar system, which countries have such as Australia which can see Stealth and some countries which have an abundance of cell phones and they can use the interference of an aircraft to find out where it is. Looking for breaking patterns and anomalies in the patterns caused by these waves and signals.

So by using a unit like this, you can draw fire from old and new technology, drive your enemy nuts, confuse them if it is a real strike because now they will not shoot until they are sure and in a real strike that could be too late. And you also save lives, save money and play hell on the logistical nightmare of competing against the United States and her military machine and next day, real-time supply chain of everything needed to fight a war. So crippling the enemies supply chain such as we did in bombing the German Factories, embargos on Iraq and the cold war with Russia was about slowing the flow of money, troops, supplies and logistics. If you run them out of weapons, most specifically SAMs, then they have nothing to fight you with. Air superiority is a given at that point.

The reason I bring this up in the increasing costs to make stealth aircraft that also perform up with the best. Wave Rider Stealth aircraft have the speed to run away from standard missiles, but a helicopter has a chance in hell of running away from a Russian or Iranian surface to air, which is shot in close proximity. Best idea is to run them out of missiles and conveniently have the factories where they are made flattened to the ground. Take out the threat early and save the money. It is low tech and high tech and fiscally responsible warfare that will mean the Military leaders are not headed off at the pass by liberal Senators who want to close bases and cut funding which kills our boys and girls in uniform.

Let's be smart when dealing with radicals. Draw their fire and then you have even more intelligence of location of fire. Number of UAVs hit or shot down, number of enemy weapons expended rounds. Think about how to kill a radical: Either

1) Make him a non-radical through a better life and education;

2.) Eliminate his ability to fight you (money or weapons);

3.) Eliminate the person from linear time. Simple really.

I hope this idea does some good to our UAV task force on Global and Universal Security of the Human Race.

UAV Targets, Aerial Dog Fights, Interception, Future of War Intelligence

The UAV, Unmanned Aerial Vehicle is hear to stay and they are rapidly replacing the glory days of the fighter pilot and soon, there will be no humans in military aircraft flying the planes. Here is a quick overview of UAVs and all the new types. Hopefully these few links can catch you up on the subject to understand the future of these units.

http://www.popsci.com/popsci/aviation/arti. ..52052- 2,00 .html

http://www.uavfomm.com/library/photo.htm

http://www.vectorsite.net/twuave.html

As you can see quite quickly there are many types of UAVs and each works on a little bit different principle of flight. Also be aware that each aircraft is a compromise, speed for stability, payload for size and power, this has always been a fact of aerospace design. Now realize that these relatively easy to build units have different functions. UAV are generally reusable but are cost effective enough that return is not as important obviously as a pilot in an F-18, Apache, A-10 etc. Even the predator costs are substantial and you do not want to lose one.

Now we know Saddam had plans for drones with cylindrical tanks for bio-toxins mounted on a aerial platform with a 14-16 foot wingspan, twin boom tail and RC devise to power it along off it's little launch pad. This is a Chemical-Biological Weapon of mass killing prototype in progress, which was a UAV project. Now then a vehicle UAV or in this case non-retrievable or it was not meant to be re-used can be made in a crude form nearly by anyone in their garage.

So how do you shoot a UAV down. Well such a large vehicle can be tracked and terminated even if the tank were plastic and the wings of wood and even little amounts of heat provides a SAM re-used or patriot a big enough foot print to intercept. But what happens when the enemy uses UAVs against us? The modern world such as the N. Koreans, Chinese, Iran all has technology that exceeds UAVs. So are we to have fighter jocks sitting in simulator type settings play aerial Mech Warrior? Perhaps, dog fighting each other.

We have done tests where a whole platoon fired at a UAV with machine guns and hand held arms and no bullets connected with the UAV at all, meaning it is hard to shoot down, hard to see and thus somewhat invisible to naked eye and footprint small enough that anything you sent after it would need rocket propellant in excess of the weight of the target and probably twice to three times the size.

Then we need newer versions of the stinger, but that means such technology will end up in the hands of Chinese who will pass it on and the arms traders will have a field day and everyone will buy weapons which can shoot down drones, UAVs and unfortunately could be used against private jets, cars, light planes and airlines, not to mention light-weight and high impact explosives to down a military jet and pilot or helicopter full of people, Humanitarian Aid or other flying machine.

Until which time it is safe to keep technology in house it might behoove people to remember that the North in the Civil war produced a muzzle spinning bullet that had better accuracy and greater range until the South got them and figured it out and produced the same, simply more blood was spilled and casualties mounted.

Same is the escalation of warfare and even though only 1 % off all the people who have ever lived have died in a war that may not mean we wish to kill off the entire race by war and keep bettering the devices of war to kill more people. However we must protect ourselves from those who differ with obvious logic thus making that argument irrelevant in nature. Sorry folks that won't happen any time soon.

So then a swarm of UAVs what are they worth. 20 stinger missiles. After all the data of troop movement could get said troops killed. Now then our goal in war is to find said enemy and eliminate threat. But if they launch UAVs we are in information damage control mode and need to get rid of the leak of information through infrared, radar, camera, heat sensors, etc, whatever the UAV is equipped with. Shooting each one down would be difficult, shooting one down is hard enough. If they send many like we are talking about doing then the problem is difficult

http://www.aerovironment.com/area-aircraft...serv/ptrdes. pdf

Now then one option not discussed anywhere I can find it is an old idea of Tesla's and ELF and it is called a ELF "SNAP" in the scientific community it refers to snapping the connection of electromagnetic energy which religious followers might call the soul. It would instantly kill all cells in the body and all the electromagnetic energy would leave instantly.

By focusing a bean or building a barrier of ELF anything flying through it would snap and all the electrical energy running any devise including the controls on the UAV would snap and the unit would harmlessly fall as soon as the fuel ran out or crash if it did not have stabilization innate tendencies through some sort of dihedral airfoils rendering it into a glider.

Now then if someone were to do this to us we would need a way to reactivate more juice, from a lead barrier which would sense no electricity and open up and restore energy, but the entire system would be blown like a fuse burned up.

However a system encased in a liquid frozen lead base would be melted by the snap and then start operating using the liquid as the generation of new power and fly on, at least you could retrieve it. And then you would know of an electro-magnetic force field barrier and avoid it with other expensive hard ware or life form such as a person. So the UAV problem is forthcoming as the technology is so readily available.

The smaller the components get and more ways they can conduct themselves and the more ways they can attain decisive military intelligence the more important it will be to terminate the enemies UAV intelligence gathering. Also of concern is the enemy feeding migratory birds food laced with RNA pathogens which do not their species making them carriers of that disease. Pathogen, virus which harms our species. Such a force field kills cells and birds on contact and their would be no more spreading to populations of friendless, or our own troops, or people.

In recap the technology has advanced enough to find a weapon against it which and where none exist, we must find a way to shoot down UAVs from our enemy. We can shoot down Drones of size, but these little things are hard to hit, the very reason we are using them besides the low cost. But the low cost makes them readily available to our enemy so then plan B must be ready now that plan A exists for all countries wishing to serve their political or radical views or will upon the freedoms and human rights owed the human race.

Scrambling frequencies is another method and taking control of their UAVs is another way with a better stronger signal once close enough. Of course we do not want them because they may contain Viruses, so we want to take control of them crash them and then put on a body suit and see what they are made of thus finding frequencies used, capabilities of frequencies, which could be used and capabilities of payload, longevity of flight, speed, and other important information. Also where the UAV was sending information too and what type of information is an important consideration.

If a UAV works on heat signatures of people or detects Co_2 coming from one's body like a mosquito finds you then. Set out thousands of little heat boxes at the body temperature or little boxes emitting Co_2 to the same amount as humans, which would show a thousand troops in an area which does not exist, misdirection leads to bad strategic moves, bad planning and good luck on our part, such the battle field changes a bit, but the basic strategy is the same and thus Von Clauswitz if alive today might ponder the same ideas if he were to know all the facts discussed.

These on-going discussions should provide the thought for research to completely figure out the possible threats and new technologies needed to keep people in the free world safe from the threat now created which is in the hands of the enemy.

Navy VTOL UAV Improvements

The US Navy is investing in VTOL UAVs, which can operate of small helipads on destroyer class or smaller ships. But will these Helicopter VTOL - Aircraft UAV combinations achieve Supersonic Flight? And will they have the manoeuverability needed to also provide stealth. In poor weather conditions and for the absolute need for BLOS information and knowledge of the enemy such UAVs might do more harm then good if they are detected as they will alert the enemy that a ship is nearby, thus making it a target and putting the ship and crew at risk of detection and attack.

Critics believe that a helicopter will never achieve supersonic Height, they say things like:—No Way! Sorry Airwolf Fans. Not possible!" They say that this is because as the helicopter has to depend on it's main rotor for lift. The problem is that as the helicopter's speed increases the retracting rotor blade (the one moving back from the direction of night) will stall and stop generating lift. When that happens the helicopter will pitch out of control and crash.

Well the US Navy thanks to some very bright aerospace engineers had figured out how to make it work. Here is the basic concept. The Being Canard Rotor/Wing Dragonfly.

http://www.vtol.org/uavpaper/Image 16. gif

In this picture we propose a three bladed symmetrical rotor blade configuration with an extremely thin and sharp leading and trailing edge, much like the F-I04. These rotor blades will stop at 350 KTS as the fuselage will fly on its own at that speed. Computer controls will prevent the flipping over warned by doubters of the innovative ability of those who know 'no-limits'.

Since there are three blades the blades will be swept forward and one will be inline with the fuselage, which can guide airflow to a single vertical stabilizer to save weight instead of the dual tail configuration here. This will allow for better manoeuverability and airflow. Since the aircraft will have short rotor blades-wings, the stress issues associated with forward swept wings will not be at issue. Here is a picture of the X-29 with forward swept wings.

http://www.dfre.nasa.gov/Gallery/Graphics/X -29/

We propose an anhedral configuration for the rotor blades and although unstable in supersonic flight the on board computer system can readjust controls 200 times a second so the problem of stability will not be an issue. The vertical stabilizer in this case can be little more than a stake on the rear of a cone as the airflow will be forcing the ram air over it. The second possibility could be a dual set of strakes coming off the round of the rear cone which attempt converge towards each other in.

The rotor blades will flow into each other at the base with a rounded convex fashion. We also propose a simple but effective thrust vectoring system, which will allow the UAV to dodge SAMs.

With these modifications we believe we can keep the UAV with an extremely tiny radar signature and maintain its stealth configuration, while allowing it to achieve supersonic flight and still operate at all speeds including a hover. We propose these changes be tested in a wind tunnel and models made to prove concept. Have drawings.

Stealth UAV High Energy Laser Reflector

In the new Net-Centric Battlespace the weapons of war

will be robotic. Many of these weapons will be energy based rather than explosives based. We are already watching new weapons both offensive and defensive weapons which include both lethal and nonlethal wave energy weapons, as well as high-energy laser weapons.

I propose that the United States of America ramp up its research and development efforts to create defensive high-energy laser weapons to protect the American People. Weapons of war so accurate and devastating that no nation will ever attempt to attack us, further I propose we design, test and build advanced stealth UAVs with high-energy chemical laser enabled platforms.

We need both and we need them now. We must develop aggressor UAVs reciprocal response weapons to attack any nation or people's who threaten our civilization. We have come too far and worked to hard to create everything we are and all we have built. From this day forward we must never choose turning a blind eye towards potential eventualities of hostile nation states, who smile for the camera and then finance International Terrorism behind our backs and the backs of our allies.

I propose that we build fast moving stealth enabled UAVs, which can fly over enemy territory or positions, flip on a beacon and allow the enemy to fire upon them. Then turn off the beacon, evade, dump chafe and then continue marking the location of the incoming SAM launch sites. Next fly to the end of the territory turn 180 degrees and fly back over those now sequenced SAM sites and targets.

The stealth UAVs will then deploy speed brakes, which will act as laser reflectors. Once the doors are open the US Net-centric Team will see them on radar and send the laser beam to them, which will be reflected downward to take out and annihilate the targets one by one in rapid sequence.

Stealth UAVs will fly in groups of three per team each three miles apart and cover a battle space grid in one pass over.

Additionally, I propose and expect to see these units available in the next major high-tech war and fully operation in the United States Military Arsenal. I believe the time for excuses is over and we must be prepared as a nation to protect the American people and not fail our duties.

Further I propose these reflector shields be made of carbon mountable and ceramic constructs and that we use these shields and new technologies be integrated into the space program for spacecraft, space stations, satellites and colonies on the Moon and Mars. Currently the United States is falling behind and not pushing the envelope on these technologies and well, we damn well should be. Think on this in 2006.

Futurist Books

- Artificial Intelligence and Possible Futures
- Comets, Asteroids, Meteorites and Earth Civilizations
- Computer Brain Interfaces of the Future
- Economics of the First Decade of the 21st Century
- Franchising the World
- Future Auto Technologies
- Future Aviation Technologies
- Future Concepts and Technology
- Future Underwater Technologies
- Growing Our Own Fuel; Switch to E85 Ethanol
- Holographic Technology of the Future
- Howerboards of the Future
- Killing Hurricanes and Weather Control

- LED Lighting of the Future
- MAV's; Micro Air Vehicle Strategies in the Future
- Killing Locust Plagues
- Pure Opinion and Politics of 2005
- Pure Opinion and Politics of 2006
- Pure Opinion and Politics of 2007
- RFID and the Future
- Robotics of the Future
- Smart Dust of the Future
- Smart Garages of the Future
- Space Colonies of the Future
- The Flow of All We Know
- The Future of High-Performance Motorcycles
- The Future of IT
- The Future Personal Tech
- The Human Animal Debate
- Truck Technologies of the Future
- UAVs of the Future
- Via Game Design Strategies for the Future
- Virtual Reality of the Future
- Wind Cars of the Future

Military Books

- Advanced Weapons Technologies of the Future
- Human Fighter Pilots Versus UAVs with AAI Computer Systems

- Robotic Net Centric Battlefield of the Future
- The Future of Military Air Superiority
- Unmanned Vehicle Robotic Warfare
- Winslow on War; Military Strategy and Philosophy
- Winslow on War; War Strategies for the 21st Century

Other Books

- Action Plan for Nairobi Slums
- ADA - Wheel Chair Awareness Plan
- An Atheist Discussion on the Absurdity of Human Religion
- Biking across America-Lower Latitudes
- Common Sense Psychology 101
- Downtown Revitalization
- Helping Out in Honduras
- Home Schooling Tips for Parents and Educators
- Honesty in Humanities
- How to Become a Writer
- How to Run a Successful Red Ribbon Week Program
- How to Run a Successful Car Wash Fundraiser
- How to Run a Neighborhood Mobile Watch Patrol
- Human Psychology of Winning
- Hypersonic Humans and Overachievers in Society
- Internet Fraud and Freedom in the Balance
- Lessons for Internet Forum Users and Bloggers
- Motivation, Goal Setting and Success Strategies

- Online Article Writing
- RV Knowledge Primer
- Social Issues of Our Time
- The Flow of Thought
- The Flow of Transportation and Distribution
- The Flow of Water
- The Hypothetical Science of Common Sense
- The Power of Presence and Brand Marketing in the 21st Century
- Think on It
- Winning Strategies for the Long-Distance Runner
- World Social Issues; Solving the Problems through Proper Planning

Business Books

- Change Management and Averting Chaos
- Customer Service Keeps Them Coming Back
- Entrepreneurial Insights for the Overachiever
- Finite Capacity Scheduling Models for Service Businesses
- Marine Industry; Things to Think about
- Marketing Magic and Market Share Management
- Non-MBA Business Management Strategies
- Over Regulation in America
- Sales Management Strategies
- Sales Training Tips from Real World

- Strategic Planning for Entrepreneurial Startups
- The Case for Off-Shoring and Outsourcing
- Understanding the Franchise Business Model

Science Fiction Books

- Alien and Human Civilizations and the Future of Inter Species Law
- The Cubed Experience
- 5u53j Son of Wilson

8

HOW JUST COULD A ROBOT WAR BE?

Just war theory is a broadly accepted theoretical framework for regulating conduct in war. It is also compatible with, if not actually a formulation of, the principles underlying most of the international laws regulating warfare, such as the Geneva and Hague Conventions.

This chapter aims to illuminate the challenges to just war theory posed by autonomous technologies. It follows Michael Walzer's [1] articulation of the theory, which has been the most influential modern text on just war theory. While there are compelling criticisms of Walzer's formulation. it is his articulation which has had the most influence on the institutions and international laws regulating war.

We should clarify what we mean by robots and other autonomous systems. "Autonomy" is a rather contentious concept, and its relation to material technologies adds further complications. It is thus useful to think about a continuum of autonomy along which various technologies fall depending upon their specific capabilities. Most generally, any system with the capability to sense. Decide and act without human intervention has a degree of autonomy. This includes simple systems, such as a landmine that "decides" to explode when it senses pressure. Obviously, systems with only the most rudimentary forms of sensors, decision processes and actions lack various aspects of full autonomy. The landmine does not decide where it will be placed, and its physical placement largely determines the consequences of its actions, thus it has much less "autonomy" than systems with more sophisticated means of sensing, deciding and acting. If we were to consider it as a moral agent, we would not be inclined to hold it morally responsible for its actions, but rather hold responsible those who placed and armed it. It thus occupies an endpoint in the continuum of autonomy and moral responsibility.

Certain kinds of "precision" weapons, such as "smart" bombs that use global positioning systems (GPS) and sophisticated control mechanisms to deliver them accurately to a target. The selection of a target, and the determination of its location, value and risks, is still determined by human agents who control the weapons system, however. Thus we might wish to "blame" a smart bomb, or its design, for failing to reach a designated target, but not for the selection of the target. It thus represents a point further along this continuum, and shares this position with various kinds of guided weapons and automated anti-aircraft batteries *(e.g.* Patriot missile systems, and the Phalanx gun systems), and automatic anti-ballistic missile systems *(e.g.* Star Wars/SDI), that detect and destroy sensed threats without immediate human intervention, though are dependent on responsible human decisions as to when it is appropriate to activate such an armed system.

Still more autonomous are systems which use sophisticated sensor analysis to select appropriate targets on their own and make decisions about the appropriateness of various actions in response to its situation. The emerging technologies of robotic weapons platforms incorporate some or all of these features, using image processing to identify targets, and selecting from a broad range of offensive and defensive actions in their engagement of targets. These are technological capabilities which already exist, and are beginning to be implemented in various countries. These systems tend to be designed to seek permission from human authorities before using lethal force against a target, what the US military calls the "human-in-the-loop," but this is not a technological necessity. We can identify the choice to use deadly force against a specific target as a critical threshold along the continuum of autonomy, and one which carries a greater moral burden in the design and use of such a technology. There are, however, systems with more autonomy than this.

As robotic technologies advance, it is possible that they will acquire moral capacities that imitate or replicate human moral capacities. While some systems might merely enact pre-programmed moral rules or principles, autonomous robotic agents might be capable of formulating their own moral principles, duties, and reasons, and thus make their own moral choices in the fullest sense of moral autonomy. There are many possibilities short of replicating a fully autonomous moral subject, such as agents with moral awareness but not the freedom of choice to act upon that awareness. While this still remains in the realm of science fiction, it is not impossible in principle that a robot could achieve autonomy in a Kantian sense, in which it takes responsibility for its actions, reasons about them morally, and identifies itself with the moral quality of its own actions. At some point along the continuum, but probably before Kantian autonomy, will arise various questions about the moral responsibilities of others towards such autonomous systems, and in particular whether these systems have moral rights.

There are many degrees of autonomy along the continuum at which specific systems might fall, so we will consider the implications of these on the interpretation and application of just war theory to various situations. I should also say something at this point about the speculative nature of this work. Many people find the idea of robotic soldiers and robotic moral agents to be somewhat fantastical, the stuff of science fiction and not something that deserves serious consideration. My arguments are meant to cover technological possibilities that do not yet exist, and even some that shall perhaps never exist, yet I believe that it is important to develop our understanding of existing technologies in light of these hypothetical possibilities. There is a very great interest in building autonomous systems of increasing complexity, and a great deal of money is being invested towards this goal. It does not seem to be an unreasonable prediction that within the next decade we will see something very much like a robotic soldier being used. If we consider the amount of time and effort it took moral and legal theorists to come to terms with the atomic bomb, then it makes sense to start thinking about military robots now, before they appear fully formed on the battlefield. Robots may not have the same potential to reshape global politics that the atomic bomb did, though indeed they may. Still, it is not unreasonable to expect that these technologies might find their way into other security applications, such as policing civilian populations. There is thus a definite necessity, and a certain urgency to establishing the moral framework in which we might judge the various applications of such technologies, as well as the ethics of designing and building them. This examination of just war theory is a part of that broader investigation.

As my concern in this analysis is with the general capabilities of technologies, primarily their ability to act autonomously, and not with the specific technologies used, I will not spend much time discussing how these technologies might work, apart from their degree of autonomy. One might also object that there already exist legal restrictions on the use of autonomous systems in combat, and these have succeeded thus far in keeping humans-in-the-loop of the most advanced military systems being developed, at least in the US, and thus there is no need for such an analysis. While it is true that humans are being kept "in the loop," it is not clear to what extent this is only a contingent truth, and whether this restriction can resist pressures to extend the autonomy granted to military systems [3]. It thus seems reasonable to review the fundamental principles which underwrite existing prohibitions on the use of autonomous technologies, as well as to try to anticipate how they may need to be augmented or extended to address new technological possibilities as they begin to appear on the horizon.

Just War Theory

Walzer's [1] just war theory aims to provide a theoretical framework for debate about the morality of specific choices and actions with regard to war by establishing a small set of principles that effectively capture general moral sentiments. Rather than dismiss all war as immoral, it seeks to carefully distinguish those specific acts that are moral so as to deny authority to those who would abuse moral sentiments in taking a nation to war, or try to legitimate immoral acts during the conduct of a war. It establishes a rational framework for distinguishing just from unjust acts of, and in, war and takes a liberal approach which seeks to protect the rights of individuals and states from unjust harms. It derives its rational principles from reflecting on shared moral sentiments and intuitions, and from recognizing the conventional nature of war and the rules of war which tend to govern it. As

McMahan [2] makes clear, there are numerous inconsistencies in how Walzer articulates the foundations of the theory in terms of individual rights, state rights, moral sentiments and conventional norms. His critique, however, aims to preserve most of the overall structure of just war theory by putting it on filmer foundations based in individual rights.

A key distinction in just war theory is drawn between what are just reasons for going to war, *jus ad bellum,* and what are just acts in the fighting of war, *jus in bello.* For Walzer, the two are completely independent of one another. Thus, for Walzer, the actions of soldiers on both sides of a war can be just if they observe the overriding principles of *discrimination* and *proportionality.* The substantive critiques of Walzer challenge this independence, and I believe that, as a moral question, proportionality depends in important ways upon the reasons for going to war. Despite this, the distinction is highly relevant to the practice and legal regulation of war and reflects two distinct moral questions, even if the moral character of how a war is fought cannot be fully determined without considering the reasons for fighting.

Autonomous Technology and *jus and bellum*

There are at least two significant ways in which autonomous technologies might influence the choice of a nation to go to war. The first of these is that such systems could directly threaten the sovereignty of a nation. As such it would challenge just war theory, or the theory might have to be extended to cover this possibility. The second way is one of the reasons many people fear the development of autonomous killing machines, like robotic soldiers, though it is not really a problem for just war theory itself. This is the belief that these technologies will make it easier for leaders who wish to start a war to actually start one, in short that autonomous technologies would lower the *barrier to entry* to war, or be directly responsible for starting a war intentionally or accidentally.

Autonomous Technologies Challenging Sovereignty

It seems that autonomous technologies offer a great potential for starting wars accidentally, and perhaps even doing so for their own purposes. While this latter potential seems more like science fiction than a real possibility, it is nonetheless useful to consider how just war theory can help aid our thinking about such a situation. The theory accepts only a few very specific causes for war as being just. In principle, only aggression against a nation's sovereignty by another nation is a just cause. Strictly speaking, the aggressor has acted unjustly and the defender has a right to self-defense, and thus may justly fight against the aggression-though history is rarely so clear cut. By extension of this principle, other third party nations may justly join in the fight on the side of nation defending itself against the aggressor, though they are not necessarily *required* to do so, *e.g.* if doing so would threaten their own existence or sovereignty. There are only a few and highly circumscribed exceptions to this principle, those being a pre-emptive strike against an immediately impending aggression, and a humanitarian intervention to stop severe human rights abuses or genocide.

With these general principles firmly in mind, we can imagine new ways in which autonomous technologies could impact upon sovereignty. First, there is the case in which an autonomous technology "accidentally" starts a war. This could be the result of human manipulation, a genuine technical error, or perhaps even by the purposeful intention of the technology. It could also turn against the nation that created it, resulting in one sort or another of a "robot revolution."

Accidental War

The idea of an "accidental" war is closely related to our conception of the sovereignty of states, though is not truly a threat to sovereignty. An "act of war" is considered to be an intentional act committed by one state against another. Thus, an unintentional act which is interpreted as an act of war could lead to an accidental war. The possibility of an accidental war has always existed, and generally the decisions to go to war are based on intentions that pre-exist any specific act of war, which is only the proximate cause or a token of justification. Autonomous technological systems introduce new dangers, however, in that they might act in unanticipated ways that are interpreted as acts of war.

There was a common fear throughout the Cold War era that the complex technological control systems for nuclear arms might malfunction, unintentionally starting a nuclear war that nobody could stop. To the extent that all large complex technological systems are prone to unpredictable errors in unforeseeable circumstances, the systems of control for autonomous robotic armies will be too. Further, to the extent that robots are used to patrol dangerous areas, contentious borders and political hot spots, it seems quite likely that some of their actions might be interpreted as acts of war, though no political or military official specifically orders such an act. While this is a real danger, it is not altogether unlike the threat posed by rogue officers and soldiers who accidentally or purposely commit such acts despite not being properly authorized by their chain of command, though they are likely to be aware of the possibilities for m is interpretation.

The wars that might result from such accidents cannot be just from the perspective of the unintentional aggressor, who then has an obligation to stand down from that aggression. While the state that is harmed by such unintentional acts has a genuine grievance, and has a right to defend itself, if it declares war in response, it will not be a just war unless the aggressor continues to pursue a war with further acts of aggression. Often, however, groups within one or both states are interested in having a war and will seize upon such incidents as opportunities to escalate hostilities and justify a full-scale war. In any case, it seems that just war theory provides the means necessary to interpret and consider cases of unintentional acts of war, in which both the human chain of command and the autonomous technology do not intend the act of war in the relevant sense.

More complex are cases in which the autonomous technologies have intentions of their own-when they are near the Kantian moral-agent end of the autonomy spectrum. Again, such agents may act unintentionally and the situation would not be unlike those in which human acts unintentionally. However, a new kind of problem arises when autonomous technologies begin to act on their own intentions and against the intentions of the states who design and use them. These situations present many problems. First, it may be difficult to distinguish a genuine intention from a technical error, which casts doubt on just what the intention behind the act is. Further, such a display of incongruent intention might indicate that the autonomous system is no longer under the control of the state, or individual, which produced or employed it. As such, it might not be appropriate to attribute its actions as being representative of the state, *i.e.* it is a rogue agent. It is not clear what responsibility a state has for the actions of rogue agents that it creates or supports, *i.e.* whether it is liable to be attacked, but the rogue agents themselves are capable of taking some of the responsibility in virtue of their moral autonomy and are certainly liable to be attacked.

These possibilities also bring into focus a new kind of question, namely whether it is wise, or just, to build and install such automated systems in the first place, given the kinds of risks they engender. This question has been asked most pointedly with automated nuclear defense systems. Here the stakes are very high, and it seems morally wrong to leave the ultimate decision to launch a nuclear assault up to an automatic process rather than a human, who might quite reasonably fail to act out of a moral sense of duty, and thus avert a total nuclear war. In fact, we might want to design military robots in a way that allows them to refuse orders that they deem to be illegal, unjust or immoral. Though researchers are only beginning to think about how we might do that.4 To the extent that autonomous systems begin acting on their own intentions, however, then we might be concerned about their acts of aggression towards their own state, as well as towards other states.

Robot Revolutions

The notion of a robot revolution is as old as the stage play in which the word "robot" was first coined, Capek's *R.UR.* [4], in which worker robots all over the world join in a global revolution and overthrow the humans. While this may seem like a fanciful bit of science fiction, we can ask serious questions about the moral status of such revolutions according to just war theory. Let us imagine a situation in which a nation is taken over by robots-a sort of revolution or civil war. Would a third party nation have a just cause for interceding to prevent this?

In such cases just war theory might be of two minds, depending upon the moral status and autonomy of the robots in question. On the one hand, it is a violation of sovereignty to interfere in the civil war of another nation. On the other hand, it is legitimate to intervene to aid a state that is being threatened by a foreign power. Thus a great deal tuns upon whether the robots who lead the revolution are seen as autonomous moral agents with a political right to revolt, or if they are the non-nitrogenous agents of some other morally autonomous agent, or if they are a non-moral or amoral system under the control of no autonomous agents but simply threaten a state. A further possibility is that the robots might represent a humanitarian crisis if they were seeking to completely eradicate or enslave the humans, though intervention would clearly be just in such a case.

Even if we consider robotic moral agents as being different than humans in important ways, the question regarding their right to revolution ultimately tums on whether they are entitled to a right to self-determination. For humans this right is tied up in other rights to individual freedom, to not be killed, to not be tortured, *etc.* While it remains to be seen if these rights are separable, due to different technological systems which only partially replicate human mental and moral capacities, we can answer this question based on the relevant portion of those rights. Assuming that we have a theory of what is required for someone to be entitled to a right to self-determination, *e.g.* a sufficiently sophisticated moral autonomy, then the robot rebels will either have this right or they will not. If they do, then just war theory will treat them just as it treats human rebels seeking to take control of their own country. If they do not, then the theory will treat them as agents of another power. If that power has legitimate claims to revolution, then there is no right for third parties to intervene. If they are agents of a foreign or otherwise illegitimate power, or of no autonomous moral agency at all—a sort of man-made disaster—then the threat they pose will justify intervention by outside powers who seek to protect the state from the robots. If in any of these cases the robots represent a humanitarian threat, then third party nations may also intervene on humanitarian grounds.

Thus we can see again that just war theory is able to deal with many of the more fanciful cases in a fairly traditional way. It leaves open, however, the critical question of whether or when machines might be due some or all of the rights of humans, as this is completely outside the scope of theory of just war. It is also not clear that it can always be easily determined whether machines are autonomous and, if not, on whose commands or intentions they are acting.

Technologically Lowering the Barriers of Entry to War

I believe that one of the strongest moral aversions to the development of robotic soldiers stems from the fear that they will make it easier for leaders to take an unwilling nation into war. This is readily apparent in light of recent history, including the 1991 Persian Gulf War, the 1999 war in Kosovo, and the 2003 invasion of Iraq. These events have brought into sharp relief the complex relationships between the political requirements on national leaders, the imagery and rhetoric of propaganda and the mass media, and the general will of citizens in the processes of deciding when a democratic nation will go to war.

Irrespective of the underlying justness of the motives, when the leadership of a state decides to go to war, there is a significant propaganda effort. This effort is of particular importance when it is a democratic nation, and its citizens disagree about whether a war is worth fighting, and there are significant political costs to a leader for going against popular sentiments. A central element of war propaganda is the estimation of the cost of war in terms of the lives of its citizens, even if that is limited to soldiers, and even if those soldiers are volunteers. A political strategy has evolved in response to this, which is to limit military involvement to relatively "safe" forms of fighting in order to limit casualties, and to invest in technologies that promise to lower the risks and increase the lethal effectiveness of their military.

We can see these motivations at work in the NATO involvement in Kosovo in 1999, in which NATO limited its military operations to air strikes. The political pressure to avoid casualties among a nation's own soldiers is thus often translated into casualties among innocent civilians, despite this being fundamentally unjust. Technologies can shift risks away from a nation's own soldiers and can thereby add political leverage in both domestic politics, through propaganda, and in diplomatic efforts to build alliances among nations. Thus, the technology functions not only in the war itself, but in the propaganda, debate and diplomacy that brings a nation into war. In this regard, it is primarily the ability of the technology to limit risks to the nation that possesses it, and its allies, that allows it to function in this way. Certainly the replacement of soldiers by robots could achieve this in a new and somewhat spectacular way, perhaps by eliminating the need for any soldiers from that nation to actually go to the battle zone.

Given these facts, it is quite reasonable to conclude that the introduction of any technology that can limit the risks to a nation's soldiers and civilians would serve a similar function. In some sense, all military technologies that work well serve this function, to some degree or when taken altogether, whether it is better airplanes, or better body armor, or better bombs, or better communications, or better strategies, or better robots, or even better battlefield surgery techniques. Indeed, recent US media has spent a great deal of energy trumpeting the technological sophistication of the US military in this way. The ultimate aim of all military technology is to give an advantage to one's own soldiers, and this means limiting their risks while making it easier to kill enemy soldiers and win the war. So in general, all military technological development aims at this same objective. Moreover, even with the most sophisticated machinery, and guarantees of extremely low casualties, most citizens in most countries are still averse to starting an avoidable war, and are nearly always averse to starting an unjust war.

Even if robots did make it easier for a nation to go to war, this in itself does not decide whether that war is just or not.

There is, however, a deeper question of political justice lurking here that concerns whether it is desirable to make it practically easier to go to war or not. If we assume that only nations fighting just wars will utilize such technologies, then it would not necessarily be unjust or immoral to develop those technologies. However, history instructs us that all wars involve at least one unjust (or badly mistaken) nation, and so the chances that such technologies will enabling future injustices is a real and legitimate concern. Moreover, it is likely that obviously just wars do not need their barriers lowered, and so this function tends to aid the propaganda of aggressors more than that of just defenders. If we agree that the majority of wars are in fact unjust on one side, then any technologies that lower the barriers to entry of war are empirically more likely to start wars period, even if one side has just cause to enter it. Still, this is an argument against militarization in general, and not specifically about autonomous systems and robots, even if they are a dramatic example of it. From an empirical perspective, it is also important to consider why these specific technologies are being heavily invested in rather than other technologies, and if it is primarily due to this propagandistic function, then this should raise concern.

Autonomous Technology and *jus in bello*

Walzer claims that just war theory is largely indifferent to the kinds of technology that are used in battle. As far as he is concerned, there are individuals who have a right not to be killed, the innocent civilians, and those who have given up that right by taking up arms, the uniformed combatants. As it is morally permissible to kill uniformed combatants, it does not matter much how one goes about killing them (assuming that one recognizes their right to surrender, *etc.)*. However, there are a number of international conventions which do limit the use of specific kinds of weapons, such as chemical, biological and nuclear weapons, as well as landmines, lasers designed to blind soldiers, and other sorts of weapons. There are various reasons for the existence of these treaties, and several principles which determine what kinds of technologies are permissible as weapons of war. In this section, we will consider how autonomous technologies might challenge the standards of *jus in bello.*

Despite Walzer's claims that his theory does not care about the technologies used for killing, he does discuss several specific technologies in terms of how they changed the conventional standards of war. In particular, the use of submarines, aerial bombing and the atomic bomb, all relatively new technologies, changed the accepted conventions of warfare during World War II.

The clearest example of this is the way in which the specific technologies of submarine warfare in World War II served to repeal a centuries-old naval warfare convention. The convention held that there was a moral duty to rescue the surviving crew of a sinking enemy ship once a battle was over. Over the long history of European naval warfare, this convention made sense to all participants, since combat usually occurred in open seas, often hundreds or even thousands of miles from safe harbors, and disabled or sinking ships generally had significant numbers of survivors. From the development of submarines through World War I, this convention held for submarines as it had for all other ships. It was decided during World War II, however, that this convention no longer applied to submarines. The reason for this was that requiring a submarine to surface and conduct rescue operations would make it too vulnerable to detection from radar and attack from airplanes armed with torpedoes. Additionally, the small submarines (with crews of less than 50) could not spare space for survivors onboard, adequate guards to take officers prisoner, or space to store much rescue equipment (ships sunk by submarines often had more than 1,000 people on board), all of which made rescue efforts challenging and impractical. They could, however, right upset lifeboats and provide food and water, as well as pick up men from the sea and put them in their own lifeboats, but these activities were considered too risky.

While there were some specific and dramatic events that led to the abandonment of this particular convention for submarines, it was largely due to the fact that obedience to the convention was so risky that it would tender submarine warfare impractical. The official abandonment of the convention occurred when the German Admiral Doenitz issued the Lacoma Order in 1942, which expressly directed submarines to not engage in any form of assistance to survivors [1]. Doenitz was tried at Nuremberg for a war crime in issuing this order, but was acquitted of the charge by the judges. The legal decision rested primarily on the fact that because both sides assented to the new convention in practice, the old convention was effectively annulled and submarines no longer had a moral obligation to rescue crews, despite the fact that it was sometimes safe for a submarine to rescue survivors. Walzer believes this is the correct moral interpretation, and accounts for it in his theory as a valid use of the principle of military necessity. That is, it became a military necessity to forgo the convention of rescue in order for submarine warfare to be an effective naval strategy, though this clearly makes naval warfare a more brutal affair.

I believe this deference to military necessity presents a significant weakness in just war theory, as formulated by Walzer, when viewed in the context of technological development. That is, why should we not say that submarines should not be used at all if they cannot be used in a manner which conforms to the conventions of just war? If we cannot argue this way, then there would seem to be a certain kind of impotence to using just war theory to argue against any technology that has the potential to change conventions via military necessity. Not only does this position mean that we have to accept all new technologies and the new conventions that arise from them, but also that. We cannot judge the morality of devising various sorts of weapons. The question is: If I can only defend myself with an indiscriminate and disproportionate weapon, because that is the only militarily effective weapon I have, then was I acting unjustly when I chose to arm myself with that weapon rather than another weapon which could be discriminate and proportionate? Do I have a moral duty to invest in weapons that will not tend to put me in positions where I may be motivated to act unjustly (indiscriminately and disproportionately) in the future? If so, could robot soldiers be such a technology?

This failure in Walzer's formulation stems from its loose foundational considerations. While Walzer is willing to assert individual rights as the basis for prohibitions against killing civilians, he mistakenly asserts that soldiers forgo their rights not to be killed by merely taking up arms. Further, he seems to believe that the restrictions on the use of weapons against soldiers, and the rights of soldiers to surrender, rescue, medical aid, etc., are a matter of convention between states who see these conventions as being in their mutual interests. Thus, there is no firm moral foundation to prevent states from abandoning these conventions when they are deemed not to be in their mutual interest. A convention depends only upon both sides assenting to it, as in Walzer's analysis of the Doenitz decision which rests upon the fact that both sides of the conflict observed the same convention.

Apart from convention, Walzer might appeal to moral sentiments in determining the morality of certain military strategies and technologies. To the extent that it derives its principles from moral sentiments, just war theory is an attempt to describe sentiments that occur after an event. In the case of many new technologies, we do not really know how that technology will function in the complex sociotechnical system of war. Submarines, radar and airplanes amed with torpedoes had never been used together in walfare before WWII, so nobody really knew how they would be used. Indeed, the German admiralty only abandoned the sea rescue convention for submarines in 1942, well into the war. Thus it seems that if we cannot predict military necessity very well, just war theory as it stands cannot tell us much about which technologies might be best left undeveloped.

The more critical issue that just war theory faces is that the conventionalist and sentimentalist interpretations both fail to secure a moral foundation for restrictions on actions against combatants *in bello*. Most generally, if we accept that the combatants on a just side of a war have not waived their rights not to be killed [2], then no conventional agreement between states can waive or trump that right. Similarly, if sailors have a moral right to be rescued after their ship is sunk, then neither the demands of military necessity, nor the technological limitations of submarines, nor the conventional agreements between belligerent navies can waive that right, even if it makes it impractical to respect it. The practicality issue comes into play only when we come to consider the legal restrictions on combat, not its fundamental morality, Thus, we might accept a certain degree of immorality in our laws because of the impracticality of judging and enforcing moral justified laws [2].

The real question then becomes one of what moral rights individuals have against the use of specific technologies, and of the moral duties of states in the development of alms that might be used in hypothetical future wars, Again there is the distinction between fundamental morality and practical law, but it seems possible in principle to develop a moral foundation for anus control and limitations on the design and use of various technologies, While it is well beyond the scope of this essay, it will remain a topic for further research.

Distinguishing Civilians & Combatants

On Walzer's interpretation of just war theory, the most fundamental distinction made by just war theory is that between combatants and civilians, While this distinction fails, like military necessity, to find solid moral grounding, it proves quite useful in establishing practical laws for regulating war. This distinction makes it legally pennissible, at least sometimes, for combatants to kill enemy combatants. It also makes it possible to say that it is almost never legally justified for combatants to kill innocent civilians, There are, of course, shades of grey. Even combatants retain certain rights, like the right to surrender, and not to be killed unnecessarily, There are also cases in which it is legally permissible to kill civilians-but these cases must meet a very strict and limiting set of conditions, and even those are contentious, Further problems arise in guerrilla and insurgent warfare, in which combatants pose as civilians.

In this section I want to consider several different aspects of the problem of distinguishing civilians and combatants as it relates to autonomous systems. First, the practical ability of autonomous technologies to draw this distinction correctly is crucial. On the one hand, it has been argued that this ability makes the use of such systems *morally required* if they are available. What is more surprising it that it is human rights groups, such as Human Rights Watch [7] in demanding the use of only "smart" bombs in civilian areas, who have made this argument. On the other hand, it is the fear of indiscriminate violence, perhaps mixed with impoverished cultural and social intelligence, that makes robotic soldiers seem particularly dangerous and morally undesirable.

The relevance of the civilian-combatant distinction to robotic soldiers is that if they are to be autonomous in choosing their targets, they will have to be able to reliably distinguish enemy combatants from civilians. It seems that this capability will remain the most difficult theoretical and practical problem facing the development of such robots. While there are technologies for picking out humans based on computer vision, motion and heat patterns, it is extremely difficult to identify particular people, or even types of people, much less to categorize them reliably into groups such as 'friend" or 'foe," the boundaries of which are often poorly defined and heavily value-laden.

In keeping with the Human Rights Watch argument, there is a line of reasoning which asserts that advanced technologies have the potential to be superior to human capabilities. Arkin [6] argues that if we can achieve the proper discriminatory capabilities in robots, they may very well be *morally superior* to human soldiers. The argument maintains that if machines are better able to discriminate civilians from combatants, then it will make fewer mistakes than humans. Moreover, because it is a machine, it will not feel the psychological and emotional stress of warfare, and thus will not be inclined to commit war crimes or atrocities as humans under such pressure might. As such, there is not only a moral obligation to use such systems when they are available, but also to build them (insofar as war is taken as an unavoidable feature of human civilization). This all depends, of course, on the actual abilities of the technology, and the abilities of combatants to fool such systems into misidentification.

"Push-Button" Wars

Walzer notes that a radical transformation in our understanding of the war convention occurred with the rise of the modern nation-state. Before this, warfare was largely conducted by individuals who freely chose to participate in a given war, and a given battle. With the rise of the modern nation-state crane the power to recruit and conscript individuals into standing armies. Because of this, nearly all individual soldiers lost their freedom to choose which wars and which battles they would fight in, even if they had the choice of whether to volunteer for military service. The consequences for moral estimations of conduct in war were thus reshaped by our knowledge that many of the actual combatants in war are not there freely, and thus deserve a certain degree of moral respect from their own commanders as well as from enemy commanders. While it is permissible to kill them, they still have the right to surrender and sit-out the rest of the war as a prisoner. It is also morally required that commanders seek out ways of winning battles that minimize killing on both sides. That is, the lives of the enemy still have moral weight, even if they weigh less than the civilians and combatants on one's own side. And the lives of one's own soldiers also count in a new way. Whereas it might be moral to lead a group of soldiers on a suicidal charge if they all volunteer for that charge, ordering conscripted soldiers into such a charge is usually immoral. In the same way, it is deemed highly honourable to throw oneself on a grenade to save one's comrades, but not to thow one's comrade onto the grenade-the autonomy of the individual soldier to choose his or her fate has moral implications.

The use of autonomous systems may similarly change our conception of the role of soldiers in war, by fully realizing a "push button" war in which the enemy is killed at a distance, without any immediate risk to oneself. This approach to war could be deemed unjust by traditional conventions of war because those doing the killing are not themselves willing to die. This principle is fundamental because it powerfully influences our sense of fairness in battle, and concerns the nature of war as a social Convention for the settling of disputes. Insofar as it can serve this purpose, both sides must essentially agree to settle the dispute through violence and, by the norms of the convention, the violence is to be targeted only at those who have agreed to fight, *i.e.* the combatants. Thus it is immoral to kill civilians, who have not agreed to fight. This convention is only abandoned in a "total war" in which no actions are considered unjust because the stakes of losing are so high. By fighting a war through pressing a button, one does not fully become a combatant because one has not conformed to the norms of war in which both sides agree to risk death in settling the dispute. The limitations of such a conventionalist notion of just war have been noted above, however, and there would seem to be no deeper moral obligation for a just combatant to risk their own lives in defense of their state.

We could imagine a war in which both sides sent only robots to do the fighting. This might be rather like an extremely violent sporting contest in which the robots destroy each other. For this to actually count as a war, and not merely a sport, however, political decisions would have to be made as a result of this competition, such as ceding territory. While it might seem unlikely that a nation would simply give up its territory or autonomy once its robots were destroyed, this is not an unreasonable or impossible outcome. It might also be deemed moral to fight to the last robot, whereas it is generally not deemed moral to fight to the last human. While many nations have surrendered after the crushing defeat of their armies but before the actual conquest of their lands, it would seem likely that a state might continue fighting with humans after its robots have been destroyed, rather than simply capitulate at that point. In general, I think it is fair to say that an exclusively robotic war might even be a highly preferable way of fighting to what now exists. In its most extreme form, we could even imagine a decisive war fought without a sieengle human casualty.

Such a war would not be completely without its costs and risks, however. First, such a war would have to take place somewhere, and it seems likely that the destruction of natural resources and civilian property would be highly likely in most locations. As the most common military objectives are to hold cities and towns, there is both the risk of harming civilians in the course of fighting, and the problems of holding towns, and thus controlling and policing civilian populations with robots. There would also be the cost in terms of the time, money and resources devoted to building up these robot armies.

At the other extreme lies the completely asymmetric "push-button" war. Thanks to science fiction and the Cold War, it is not hard to imagine an autonomous military system in which the commander needs only to specify the military action, and press a button, the rest being taken care of by a vast automated war machine. We could even imagine a civilian government that has completely replaced its military with a fully automated system, perhaps designed and staffed by civilian technicians, but one that did not require any uniformed soldiers to operate. Such a system would, I believe, seriously challenge the conventional concept of war.

In a completely asymmetric war, in which one side offers no legitimate uniformed combatants in battle, but only robots, our moral sentiments could be profoundly upset. If one nation fights a war in which its soldiers never appear on the battlefield, offering no opportunity for them to be killed, then the combatants are all machines and the humans are all civilians. As in a guerrilla war, one side presents no legitimate human targets to be killed. A legitimate army would not have any opportunity to reciprocally kill the soldiers of their opponents in such a situation (and could only inflict economic damage on their robots). This could thereby be interpreted as a fundamental violation of the war convention itself, like showing up for a duel in armor or sending a proxy, and thereby as a nullification of the associated conventions. Seen another way, such a situation might also be presented as an argument in favor of terrorism against the civilians who sit behind their robotic army. It could be argued that because such an army is the product of a rich and elaborate economy, the members of that economy are the next-best legitimate targets. This possibility should alert us to unsuitability of conventions and moral sentiments, rather than individual rights, as a basis for just war theory, since we would not want a theory of just war which legitimizes terrorism.

If we instead see the foundations of just war as deriving from individual rights, it would be unreasonable to insist that a nation fighting for a just cause is obliged to let an unjust aggressor kill its citizens even though it has the technological means of preventing this. Indeed, outside of Walzer's interpretation of the moral equality of soldiers, we do not expect a technologically superior nation to refrain from using its available technologies simply because they give too great of an advantage, nor do we expect a larger army to use special restraint in fighting a smaller army out of a moral sense of fairness. Similarly, as long as the robot army is no more likely to cause unjust harms than a human army, it would seem to offer a superior military advantage in limiting the risks to one's own citizens.

There is a compelling rationale for a nation desiring to defend itself without risking human lives. That is, a nation could quite reasonably decide that it does not want its children to be trained as soldiers or sent to war, and so develops a technological solution to the problem of national defense that does not require human soldiers, namely a robot army. In such a case it would not seem to be immoral to develop and use that technology, and we might go even further and say it is morally required for that nation to protect its children from becoming soldiers if it is within their technological capacity to do so. If an aggressor invaded this nation, I do not think many people would raise a moral objection to their using robot soldiers to defend themselves.

Of course, the push-button war is already available in a certain sense, namely for those countries with superior air forces and a willingness to bomb their enemies. The practical consequence of such wars is the asymmetric war in which one side is so obviously technologically powerful that it does not make much sense for the opposition to face it in the traditional manner. The result is often guerrilla warfare, and sometimes terrorism. The advent of robot armies may further exacerbate such situations, but would not seem to be fundamentally different. Their development and employment should, however, take into consideration that these are likely responses to the use of robot armies, even if they are not morally just responses.

Conclusions

Ultimately, just war theory concludes that the use of autonomous technologies is neither completely morally acceptable, nor is it completely morally unacceptable under Walzer's [I] interpretation of just war theory. In part this is because the technology, like all military force, could be just or unjust, depending on the situation. This is also, in part, because what is and is not acceptable in war, under this interpretation, is ultimately a *convention,* and while we can extrapolate from existing conventions in an attempt to deal with new technologies, like autonomous killing machines, this process can only be speculative. It is up to the international community to establish a new set of conventions to regulate the use of these technologies, and to embody these in international laws and treaties. Such a process can be informed by Walzer's theory, but his approach is to appeal to conventional practices as the ultimate arbiter of military necessity when it comes to technological choices. In light of this, we may wish to extend or revise the theory of just war to deal more explicitly with the development and use of new military technologies. In particular, we might seek to clarify the moral foundations for technological arms control, perhaps upon individual rights or another solid moral ground. Such a theory might also begin to influence the practical control of autonomous weapons systems through international laws and treaties. I believe that this would be a promising approach for further work.

REFERENCES

1. M. Walzer, *Just and Unjust Wars: A Moral Argument with Historical Illustrations,* Basic Books, NY, 1977.
2. J. McMahan, The Sources and Status of Just War Principles, *Journal of Military Ethics,* 6(2), 91 106, 2007.
3. J. S. Canning, A Concept of Operations for Armed Autonomous Systems: The difference between "Winning the War" and "Winning the Peace", presentation at the Pentagon. 2007.
4. K. Capek. *Russum's Universal Robots (RUR),* 1921.
5. L. Alexander, The Doomsday Machine: Proportionality, Prevention and Punishment. *The Monist,* 63,199-227,1980.
6. R. C. Arkin, Governing Lethal Behavior: Embedding Ethics in a Hybrid Deliberative/Reactive Robot Architecture, Georgia Institute of Technology. Technical Report GIT -GVU-07-11, 2007.
7. Human Rights Watch, International Humanitarian Law Issues in the Possible US Invasion of Iraq, *Lancet,* Feb. 20, 2003.

BIBLIOGRAPHY

Davi S.A. : Tele Communications and Politics. The Secentralised Alternative, London, Pinter 1994.

Friedman, G. : The Future of War : Power, Technology and American World Dominance in the 21st century, N.Y., Random House, 1996.

Holsti–The State, War and the State of War, Cambridge, Cambridge Univ. Press. 1996.

Posen, B.R. : The Sources of Military Doctrine, Ithaca 1984, Cornell Univ. Press.

Posen, P. Societies and Military Power : India and its Armies, Ithaca, Cornell University Press, 1996.

Friedman, G. : The Future of War : Power, Technology and American World Dominance in the 21st Century, N.Y. Random House, 1996.

Huntigton, S.P. : The Soldier and the State, N.Y. Vintage Books, 1964.

Bellamy, C. : Knights in White Armour : The New Art of War of Peace, London, Random House, 1997.

Mary W. Asian Power and Politics : The Cultural Dimension of Authority, Cambridge Belknap Press, 1985.

INDEX

■■■